# HOW TO
# REPLACE & INSTALL
# DOORS & WINDOWS

*T1-BIZ-781*

Created and designed
by the editorial staff
of ORTHO Books

| | |
|---|---|
| Project Editor | Sally W. Smith |
| Writer | T. Jeff Williams |
| Designer | Jacqueline Jones |
| Illustrators | Ron Hildebrand |
| | Ronda Hildebrand |

D0608197

# Ortho Books

**Publisher**
Robert L. Iacopi

**Editorial Director**
Min S. Yee

**Managing Editors**
Anne Coolman
Michael D. Smith
Sally W. Smith

**Production Manager**
Ernie S. Tasaki

**Editors**
Jim Beley
Susan Lammers
Deni Stein

**Design Coordinator**
Darcie S. Furlan

**System Managers**
Christopher Banks
Mark Zielinski

**Photographic Director**
Alan Copeland

**Photographers**
Laurie A. Black
Richard A. Christman

**Production Editors**
Linda Bouchard
Alice Mace
Kate O'Keeffe

**Asst. System Manager**
William F. Yusavage

**Chief Copy Editor**
Rebecca Pepper

**Photo Editors**
Anne Dickson-Pederson
Pam Peirce

**National Sales Manager**
Garry P. Wellman

**Sales Associate**
Susan B. Boyle

**Operations Director**
William T. Pletcher

**Operations Assistant**
Gail L. Davis

**Administrative Assistant**
Georgiann Wright

Address all inquiries to
Ortho Books
Chevron Chemical Company
Consumer Products Division
Box 5047
San Ramon, CA 94583

First Printing in March, 1984

8  9  10
90  91  92  93  94

ISBN 0-89721-023-9

Library of Congress Catalog Card
Number 83-62650

## Chevron Chemical Company
6001 Bollinger Canyon Road, San Ramon, CA 94583

No portion of this book may be
reproduced without written permission
from the publisher.

We are not responsible for unsolicited
manuscripts, photographs, or
illustrations.

Every effort has been made at the time
of publication to guarantee the
accuracy of the names and addresses
of information sources and suppliers
and in the technical data contained.
However, the reader should check for
his or her own assurance and must be
responsible for selection and use of
suppliers and supplies, plant materials
and chemical products.

## Acknowledgments

### Architects and Designers

*Front cover, back cover, pages 44, 46-47:* Robert A. M. Stern, New York, NY

*Page 1:* Amick & Harrison, San Francisco, CA

*Pages 4, 48, 49, 72:* James Cutler, Winslow, WA

*Page 20 (lower left):* Lorenz & Williams, Dayton, OH

*Page 20 (lower right):* Alice Roedersheimer, A.S.I.D., Dayton, OH

*Page 42:* Jacobson, Silverstein, Winslow, Berkeley, CA

*Page 45:* Obie Bowman, Sea Ranch, CA

### Photography

*Front cover, back cover, pages 44, 46-47:* © Sepp Seitz / Woodfin Camp & Associates

*Pages 1, 4, 16, 19 (upper right), 19 (lower right), 20 (top), 42, 48, 49 (top), 72:* Laurie A. Black

*Pages 18, 20 (lower left), 20 (lower right), 21:* Susan Lammers

*Page 19:* E. Alan McGee/FPG

*Page 45:* Obie Bowman

*Page 49 (bottom):* James Cutler

### Special Thanks to:

Blair Abee
Batey & Mack
John and Sherry Bennett
Julie Erreca
Dr. and Mrs. John D. Bullock
Dr. and Mrs. Daniel Camacho
Mr. and Mrs. Steven A. Cooper
Judith Epstein
Barbara Ferguson
Fisher-Friedman Associates
Kathy Hadley
Steve and Patsy Larson
Mr. and Mrs. L. T. Loberg
Iver and Terry MacDougall
Mr. and Mrs. Donald M. Miller
Doug Rice
Mr. and Mrs. Chas. Roedersheimer
Susan Young

### Consultants

Bob Beckstrom
Berkeley, CA

Bill Eggers
San Anselmo, CA

Eric Ekstrom
National Woodwork
    Manufacturers Association
Park Ridge, IL

John Gurniak
Architectural Aluminum
    Manufacturers Association
Chicago, IL

John Johnson
San Anselmo, CA

Raymond Moholt
Fir and Hemlock Door
    Association
Portland, OR

### Editorial Assistance

Beverley DeWitt
Karin Shakery

### Copyediting and Proofreading

Editcetera
Berkeley, CA

### Graphic Design Assistants

Mary Lynne Barbis
Susan Bard
Laurie Phillips

### Typesetting

George Lithograph
San Francisco, CA

### Color Separation

Color Tech
Redwood City, CA

## Front and Back Covers

Doors and windows occupy most of the rear facade of this shingled beach house. On the main floor, pairs of glass-inset doors flank a pyramid of square windows. In the master bedroom above, a magnificent half-round window follows the curve of a vaulted ceiling. By day or by night, the drama of doors and windows draws one's eye. For an interior view of the bedroom, see page 44; the dining area, on the left end of the ground floor, is shown on pages 46-47.

## Page 1

Doors and windows of industrial steel open onto a deck from a dining area. Custom-made to fit a wall that previously held only a smaller window, they render the division between indoors and outdoors nearly invisible. Traditional French doors have smaller, wood-framed panes of glass (see page 20 for an example); here, the spare utilitarian quality of the metal framing is appropriate to the contemporary style of the house.

# HOW TO REPLACE & INSTALL DOORS & WINDOWS

## Door & Window Construction Basics  5

Building a New Wall  6
Cutting an
    Opening in a Wall  10

## Doors  17

Types of Doors  22
Installing a Prehung Door  24
Hanging Your Own Door  26
Double Doors  30
Storm & Screen Doors  31
Sliding Glass Doors  32
Pocket Door  34
Bifold Doors  36
Sliding Closet Doors  37
Doorknobs & Locks  38
Door & Window Trim  40

## Windows  43

Choosing the Right Window  50
Removing an
    Existing Window  52
Fixed-Pane Window  54
Wood-Framed Window  58
Metal-Framed Window  60
Greenhouse Window  61
Skylight  62
Bay Window  68

Index  94
Metric Chart  96

## Maintenance & Repair  73

Sealing the House  74
Replacing Glass &
    Repairing Screens  82
Solving Door Problems  84
Treating Window Pains  89
Repainting
    Doors & Windows  92

# DOOR & WINDOW CONSTRUCTION BASICS

Framing a door or window opening is easy
when you understand the anatomy of
a stud wall. Whether you're working on
new construction or a remodeling project,
this chapter shows you how
to frame the door or window opening you need.

The doors and windows in your house do more than just admit light and people; they set the tone, in both appearance and function, for the entire house. An entrance door, whether elaborate Victorian, solid oak with brass strap hinges, leaded glass, or elegantly paneled, makes a statement about the style of the house. Windows, too, shape the effect your house has, giving it an air of formality, perhaps, or balanced symmetry, or whimsical variety. Whether you are building a house, remodeling part of your home, or just trying to maintain it in good condition, don't overlook the possibilities that doors and windows offer.

Replacing old doors and windows will dress up an older house and contribute to lower heating and cooling bills. It's also wise. Your house represents a sizable investment, and that undoubtedly means you want to maintain its quality.

You will save about half the cost of replacing or installing doors or windows by doing the work yourself, which is what this book is all about. Replacing a front door with a new one the same size involves only a few hours' work, and will markedly improve the house's appearance. Replacing old, drafty windows with new double-pane thermal windows shows immediate savings on energy bills.

In the house opposite, doors and windows line a grassy courtyard. (An exterior view appears on page 48.) The large expanse of glass, which takes advantage of a southern exposure, was carefully designed to allow the use of standard 76-inch-high glass panels. To increase the flow of space between the indoors and the outdoors, the fir-framed doors were specially milled to conform to the same height. Installing window walls such as these requires careful construction of door and window openings to maintain the load-bearing capacity of the wall.

Numerous ways to improve your house with new doors and windows are explored in this book, including how to put in a door where none now exists. Perhaps you think that tearing out a wall is too big a job for a do-it-yourselfer. You'd be surprised. One of the best-kept secrets among carpenters is how easy it is to frame walls—you just need to know the basics. This book details every necessary step in opening a wall, providing the proper structural support, and putting in a new doorway or window wherever you want it. If you can hammer a nail and saw a board, you can do the job.

Even if you aren't ready for installing a new door or window just now, this book shows you how to keep what you have in good working order, including how to fix stuck windows and warped doors and how to weatherstrip them to cut costly infiltration of the cold of winter or heat of summer. When it comes to repair and maintenance, all you have to do is get started.

## Building Permits

You need a building permit if you make any structural changes in your house. If you take off a door and put in a new one the same size or if you replace a window with one the same size, you probably don't need a permit. But altering the size of the opening or cutting a new one are structural changes, and you will need a permit.

Permits are obtained from the building inspector's office. You need to draw a detailed plan of your construction changes showing the proposed height and width, and a proper-sized header, or support beam, above the door or window opening. Details on the proper-sized header, determined by your opening's span, are given on page 8. You can use the drawings of door or window openings shown in the book to make your own plans. If any plumbing or wiring must be relocated when cutting a new opening in the wall—see page 12 for information—include the details in your plan. You must obtain separate plumbing and wiring permits. Permits cost you a little money and time, but they ensure that no weaknesses will develop in the wall (or roof, for a skylight) that could endanger you and your family.

# BUILDING A NEW WALL

To fully understand the process of installing a door or window, you need to know the basics of stud wall construction. With this knowledge, you can put up divider walls, complete with doors and windows. If you open up a wall of your house to put in a door or window, you will understand how that framework—the stud wall—behind the surface of the wall is assembled. This section deals with how a stud wall is constructed, including door and window openings in it. Before attempting to open a wall, be sure to read pages 10–11 carefully, since different types of house construction call for different support systems in the stud wall.

## Laying Out the Stud Wall

The basic framework of a house is made up of stud walls. They are usually made of 2-by-4 lumber, although some houses use 2 by 6s. In building a stud wall, use lumber stamped "stud grade" or "standard or better." Building codes forbid you to use the cheaper and weaker grades of lumber.

The stud wall consists of the sole plate at the bottom, the vertical studs, the top plate at the top, and the overlaying cap plate, often called the double top plate.

Let's assume you would like to put a wall across one end of your garage, including both a door and a window. (For a detailed description on how to put four walls together, topped with a roof, see Ortho's book, *Basic Carpentry Techniques.*)

Each end of the divider stud wall must be anchored by nailing it to studs in the existing walls. Select those studs, then measure the width of the room between the studs to find the length of your divider wall. If necessary, remove any baseboards so the new wall will fit flush against the existing wall. Cut two 2 by 4s to the proper length and lay them flat, side by side on the floor. One is the sole plate and the other is the top plate.

The next step is to determine exactly where each stud is to be nailed. If you must use two boards for each plate, make sure that the butt joint in the top plate is offset by at least 4 feet to the right or left of the joint in the cap plate, and that any joint in the top plate is centered over the end of a stud (see illustration).

Studs are usually laid out 16 inches apart as measured from the center of one stud to the center of the other. In some cases, the studs are 24 inches apart; the following discussion is based on 16-inch spacing, which is termed *on 16" centers* and is written *16" o.c.*, or *16" on center.* This spacing provides both structural strength and the proper placement for attaching 4-foot-wide exterior paneling or interior wallboard—the edge of a panel will fall in the center of a stud.

To lay out the stud positions, hook your tape over the end of the sole plate and mark every 16 inches. If the last stud ends up only a few inches from the end stud, so be it. Don't leave it out.

All studs must be centered over the 16-inch mark. But when you put a stud on that line, it will cover the mark so you can't precisely center it. Here's a trick from the pros: at each 16-inch mark, back up ¾ inch, which is half the width of a stud,

**Stud wall construction**

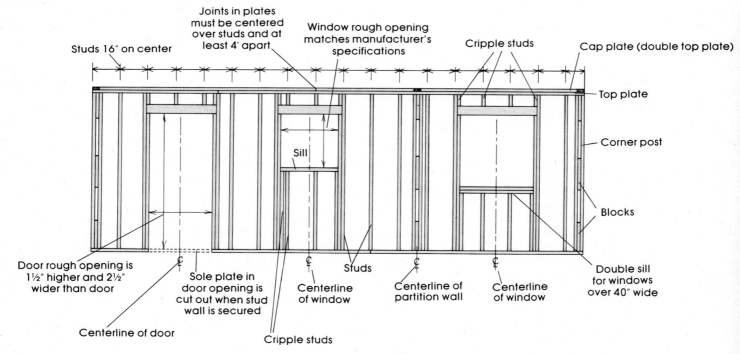

Studs 16" on center

Joints in plates must be centered over studs and at least 4' apart

Window rough opening matches manufacturer's specifications

Cripple studs

Cap plate (double top plate)

Top plate

Corner post

Sill

Blocks

Door rough opening is 1½" higher and 2½" wider than door

Sole plate in door opening is cut out when stud wall is secured

Centerline of door

Cripple studs

Centerline of window

Studs

Centerline of partition wall

Centerline of window

Double sill for windows over 40" wide

and mark there. Use your square to draw a line across the sole plate through that mark. The edge of the stud is aligned with that mark. Put a large *X* beside the line to remind yourself which side of the line the stud goes on.

Once you have marked one plate, put the other beside it, make sure both ends are even, and use your square to draw the stud alignment marks across both at once, as illustrated. Don't forget to place the *X*s where the studs go.

### Corners

If you are putting two walls together at right angles, start measuring wall B from the outside corner of wall A, as illustrated. This way the leading edge of a 4-by-8 panel of plywood or drywall will be centered on a stud.

You also need to know how to make a corner stud. It is done simply by sandwiching three 12-inch to 18-inch pieces of 2 by 4 between two studs, as illustrated. Only one wall has a corner stud; it doesn't matter which one. The other wall simply has an end stud, which is nailed to the corner stud when both walls are up and in place.

## Assembling the Stud Wall

Once the top and bottom plates have been marked, you are ready to put the wall together. The instructions that follow show you the mechanics of nailing together a stud wall. But before actually doing it, read through both this and the following section on framing door and window openings.

To put a wall together, stand the top plate and sole plate on edge, with the markings facing each other, and separate them by the length of the studs. Put the studs in place over the *X*s with their edges along the lines. The end studs, or corner stud if two walls join at right angles, should be flush with the ends of the plates. Stand with one foot on a stud and drive two 16-penny (16d) nails through the plate into the end of each stud. That's it. The cap plate, or double top plate, goes on after the wall is up.

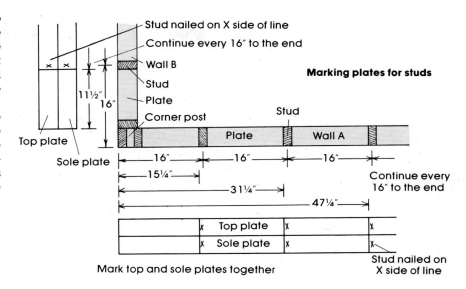

**Marking plates for studs**

Mark top and sole plates together

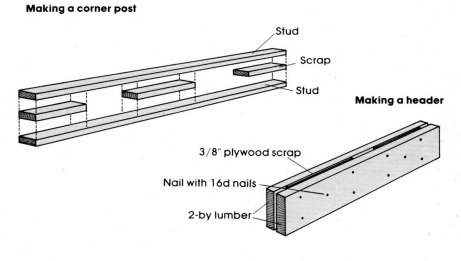

**Making a corner post**

**Making a header**

3/8" plywood scrap
Nail with 16d nails
2-by lumber

**Nailing the stud wall together**

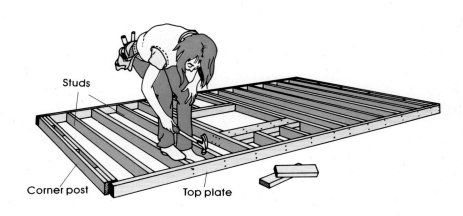

### Framing a Door or Window Opening

Now that the mysteries of a stud wall have been revealed, have a look at how to frame a door or window opening.

A door or window opening in a wall means there will be no stud support there. To prevent the top plates from bowing under the weight of the roof and ceiling joists, *headers* (also called *lintels*) must be installed. Headers are usually constructed from 2-by lumber cut the width of the opening. They must always be placed on edge; to make them the same width as the studs, a strip of ⅜-inch plywood is always sandwiched between the two pieces. (Some construction books tell you to use ½-inch plywood, but this is a little too wide.)

For structural strength, headers must be a certain size, depending on the width of the opening. In planning header sizes for a one-story house, follow this span chart (for more than one story, check your local code):

| Opening | Header Size |
|---|---|
| up to 4' across | 2 × 4s |
| up to 6' across | 2 × 6s |
| up to 8' across | 2 × 8s |
| up to 10' across | 2 × 10s |
| up to 12' across | 2 × 12s |

The space between the header, which is fitted right above the door or window, and the top plate must be filled with *cripple studs* spaced 16 inches on center, in the same location full-sized studs would be placed.

A footnote on headers: in a major construction project, it is time-consuming to build the headers, then cut and fit the cripple studs above them. Instead, the pros generally use 4 by 12s for all headers. The header is cut to the proper length, snugged up against the top plate, and the trimmer studs nailed in place to support each end. All doors and windows are thus at the same height automatically, and the header (actually 11¼ inches high) provides enough room for all door and window jambs.

### Doors

Study the drawing of the door opening and become familiar with the king studs, trimmer studs (also called jack studs), header, and cripple studs. Standard construction uses doors 80 inches high and places the tops of all windows at the same level. The layout procedure described here allows for an 80-inch-high door.

The rough framed opening should be 1½ inches higher than the height of the door and 2½ inches wider than the door. This additional clearance allows for the door jamb material, whether you have a prehung door unit or are building your own door jambs, and for adjusting the fit. The framing procedure is the same for both exterior and interior doors.

Here's how to frame the rough door opening. Use an existing stud as a king stud if it is close to where you want the door opening. Cut a trimmer stud 80 inches long and nail it to the king stud and through the sole plate.

Measure the width of the door, plus 2½ inches, plus an additional 1½ inches for the width of the trimmer stud, and nail another king stud there. Nail an 80-inch-long trimmer stud to the second king stud on the inside of the opening.

Next, place the header on edge so it rests on top of the trimmer studs and nail through the king studs into the ends of the header. Measure and cut cripple studs. Place one over each trimmer stud above the header against the king studs and the rest on the 16-inch center marks on the top plate. Nail them through the top plate and toenail the bottoms to the header.

After the wall is up and complete, cut away the sole plate in the door opening. It will now be 81½ inches high, just right for the door and jamb.

**Door framing**

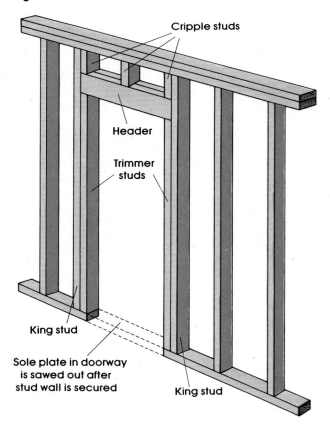

Cripple studs

Header

Trimmer studs

King stud

Sole plate in doorway is sawed out after stud wall is secured

King stud

## Windows

A window opening is constructed much like a door opening with one big difference: a window fits into the opening with only ¼ inch to ½ inch clearance on all sides. Because a window frame is much stronger than a door and jamb unit and not so likely to slip out of square, it is shimmed only under the bottom edge, to make it level.

Just like a door, a window fits into an opening comprised of king studs, trimmer studs, a header, and cripple studs. The major additions are a rough sill and cripple studs underneath to support the window.

Here's the method for constructing a window opening. Determine the size of the rough opening: the window's dimension plus ¼ inch to ½ inch on all sides, or the manufacturer's specifications. Use an existing stud for one of the king studs, or nail a new king stud in place, if necessary. Mark both plates (sole and top) for the second king stud by measuring away from the first one the rough opening width plus 3 inches (for two trimmer studs). Nail the second king stud in place.

Install the header at the same height as the door headers by marking both king studs 80 inches from the top of the sole plate. Place the bottom of the header at the marks and drive five 16d nails into each end through the king studs.

Cut two trimmer studs 80 inches long. Mark the trimmers for the rough sill by measuring down from their tops the height of the rough opening (plus 1½ inches if the rough sill will be double). Cut a rough sill to the rough opening width; place it between the trimmers. Line up its top with the marks and nail two 16d nails through the trimmer into each end.

Nail the trimmer-and-sill assembly to the king studs with 16d nails. Drive two 16d nails through the sole plate into the end of each trimmer.

Measure and cut cripple studs to fit between the sole plate and rough sill. Nail them with two 16d nails through the sole plate and rough sill. If the rough sill is double, measure and cut the second sill and nail it to the first with 16d nails.

Measure and cut cripple studs to fit between the top plate and header. You will have to toenail their bottoms into the header. The two sets of cripple studs should be vertically aligned on the 16-inch-center stud layout pattern for the wall. Be sure to place cripple studs next to the trimmer studs.

## Completing the Stud Wall

To continue with the example of a divider wall installed between two existing walls: You now have the stud wall ready to be raised into place. Snap a chalkline across the floor where you want one edge of the sole plate to line up. Note that the end studs of the new wall should be centered on studs in the existing walls to provide a nailing base. With one or more helpers, raise the new wall and align the sole plate on the chalkline. Nail the sole plate to the floor between the studs. For concrete floors, use case-hardened concrete nails.

There is no cap plate on this wall because if you had put it on while the wall was on the floor, the new wall would have jammed against the ceiling as it was raised.

Before putting the cap plate in place, use a level to make sure the wall is plumb (vertical), then nail the end studs to the studs in the existing walls. Slip the cap plate in place and nail it twice: First nail through the underside of the top plate between the studs to secure it; then, after you have double-checked again that the wall is plumb, toenail the cap plate to the ceiling joists. Find the joists by rapping on the ceiling. Joists are normally spaced 24 inches on center.

Where two walls are joined together at a corner, the cap plate of one wall overlaps the top plate of the other wall to tie them together.

**Window framing**

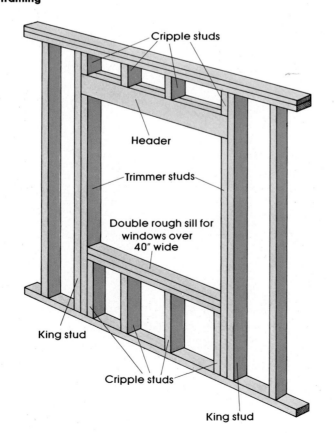

Cripple studs

Header

Trimmer studs

Double rough sill for windows over 40" wide

King stud

Cripple studs

King stud

# CUTTING AN OPENING IN A WALL

## Preparing for the Opening

If you have never cut into a house wall, you'll feel a bit like a rookie brain surgeon. It can be a little scary—"Don't cut *there*, dear!"—but it's done all the time. Just carefully plan ahead. Besides, once there is a big saw cut in your favorite wall, a certain fatalistic pleasure creeps in. You know you can't turn back.

Use the steps below for houses sheathed in wood, aluminum, vinyl, or stucco. To open a brick or concrete block wall, consult a contractor or a structural engineer.

### Platform or Balloon Framing

Up until the early 1930s, houses were commonly constructed in what is called balloon framing. After that, builders generally switched to the more efficient platform, or Western, framing. However, some houses even today are built with balloon framing. Before you cut a hole in your wall and remove any supporting studs, you need to determine which style was used in your house. When cutting a new opening, balloon framing requires more ceiling and wall support than does platform framing.

From the illustrations you can see the basic differences. In balloon framing there are no top and bottom plates. Instead, the studs run the full height of the wall, and the ceiling joists are supported on a ledger board called a ribbon that is set into the studs. In platform style, the subfloor rests on floor joists and the stud wall rests on the subfloor.

You can determine the construction style in the crawl space or basement under the house. Under the house, in balloon framing, the ends of studs rest directly on the mudsill (redwood or treated board), which is fastened to the top of the foundation, and these studs are nailed to the floor joists. In platform framing, the floor joists rest on the mudsill, and there are no studs beside them, only the subfloor attached directly to the joists.

However, if your house is built on a slope, look carefully. You may see what appear to be studs in balloon framing, but they are, in fact, probably cripple studs that fill the gap between the low end of the foundation and the level floor. In platform framing those studs will have a doubled plate on top, with the floor joists resting on the cap plate. In balloon framing the studs will pass beyond the first and upper floor joists, which will be resting on a ribbon (ledger board) that is set into the studs.

### Bearing or Nonbearing Wall

A bearing wall carries the weight of the roof, ceiling joists, or both if it is an exterior wall. Walls with eave overhangs on the outside are bearing walls, supporting the roof rafters. Walls at the gable ends of the house generally are not bearing walls. Any wall that supports ceiling joists or rafter ends must be considered a bearing wall, so go up in the attic and have a look when in doubt. Use the illustration, which shows typical ceiling joist layouts, to

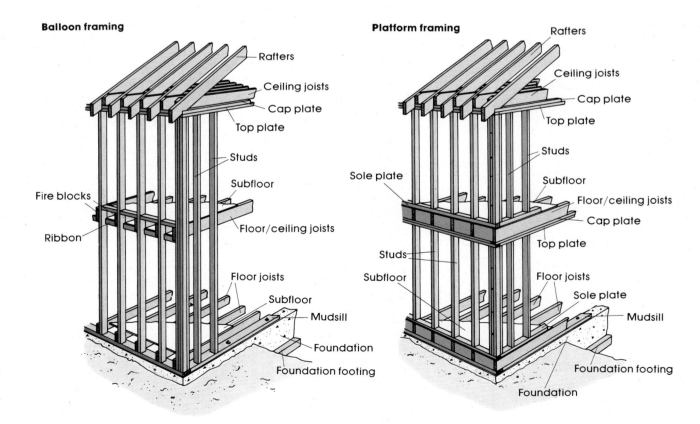

**Balloon framing**

Rafters
Ceiling joists
Cap plate
Top plate
Studs
Subfloor
Floor/ceiling joists
Fire blocks
Ribbon
Floor joists
Subfloor
Mudsill
Foundation
Foundation footing

**Platform framing**

Rafters
Ceiling joists
Cap plate
Top plate
Studs
Subfloor
Floor/ceiling joists
Cap plate
Top plate
Sole plate
Studs
Subfloor
Floor joists
Sole plate
Mudsill
Foundation footing
Foundation

help ascertain your own situation.

The simplest wall to open up is a nonbearing wall in a platform-framed house. The most difficult, but certainly in the range of the handy do-it-yourselfer, is a bearing wall in a balloon-framed house. It just takes an extra support system.

### Ceiling-Support Systems

When cutting an opening in a bearing wall, you must support the ceiling joists while you work, or the weight of the roof and ceiling joists may bow the wall. In a balloon-style house, you must have two support systems. Before erecting the support system, locate your planned opening (page 13).

**Platform-style House.** For an opening in the wall of a platform-framed house, the ceiling is supported by a temporary studwall erected about 4 feet back from the wall to be cut. This supports the joists while still giving you room to work. Construct it just like you would a standard stud wall (pages 6–9), and make it 4 feet wider than the planned opening. Center it on the opening.

Nail the support wall together, stand it in place, then have some friends steady it while you slip in the cap plate. Drive shims—some shingles—from both sides between the top plate and the cap plate under each ceiling joist to press the support wall into position. As long as the cap plate doesn't slip, it should not mar the ceiling, but if in doubt allow a little extra room for cushioning material between the plate and ceiling.

**Balloon-style House.** In a balloon-framed house, first support the ceiling as described above. Then, after removing the interior wall covering for the rough opening, tack a 2 by 8 to the studs tight against the ceiling, as shown. It should reach completely across the planned door or window opening. This is called a *whaler.* Drill holes through it into each stud and tighten it in place with ⅜-inch by 4-inch lag screws. For extra support, cut a 2 by 4 to fit snugly under each end of the whaler. You can now remove the studs from the opening.

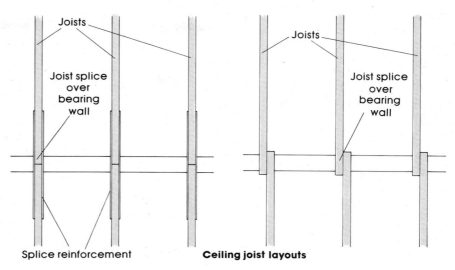

Splice reinforcement    **Ceiling joist layouts**

**Support system for platform-style house**

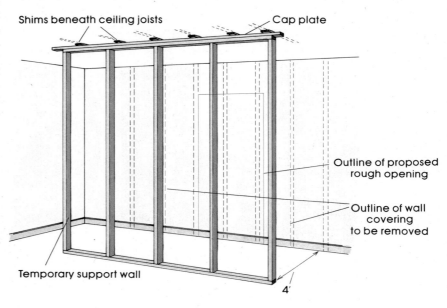

Shims beneath ceiling joists    Cap plate

Outline of proposed rough opening

Outline of wall covering to be removed

Temporary support wall    4'

**Support system for balloon-style house**

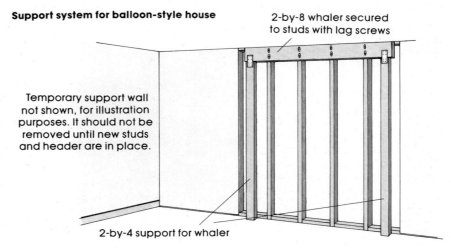

2-by-8 whaler secured to studs with lag screws

Temporary support wall not shown, for illustration purposes. It should not be removed until new studs and header are in place.

2-by-4 support for whaler

### Electrical Wires

Chances are high that you will find electrical wires in any wall you cut. Generally, the wires run across the wall in holes drilled in the studs between 1 foot and 3 feet from the floor. If you are making a fairly high window opening, you may not have to reroute wires, but for many windows and any door opening, you will. *Before you cut into a wall, be sure the electricity to that area is shut off.* Double-check by plugging a lamp into the wall outlet. (To run your electric tools, you may have to run extension cords from elsewhere in the house.)

There are two standard kinds of wiring; your house will likely have one of these. In older houses you may find two black insulated wires running side by side. More recent wiring has a single plastic-coated cable that contains three wires. Whatever you have, take a sample to your hardware store and buy material that matches it. Purchase enough wire to reach from the floor on one side of the opening to the ceiling, across the opening, and down to the floor on the other side. Add a couple more feet to be sure you have enough.

The problem here is how to connect the wires on each side of the opening. It is against the National Electrical Code simply to twist them together, or even to join them within a junction box inside the wall, since you always must have access to a junction box.

The solution is to install a receptacle on each side of the opening. If the new opening is in an exterior wall, one of the outlets can be placed on the outside of the house. In this case the National Electrical Code requires that you use a Ground Fault Circuit Interrupter (GFCI) receptacle on the outside. For complete information on installing outlets and GFCIs, see Ortho's book, *Basic Wiring Techniques*.

From the illustration you can see that the wires are connected in one receptacle, run up and over the header of a door or window opening through holes drilled in the studs and cripple studs, then down to the receptacle on the other

side. Alternatively, you can run the wires under the doorway by drilling through the sole plate, through the floor joists, and through the sole plate on the other side.

Note that in old house wiring, where you have only two insulated wires, there is no ground wire.

### Plumbing Pipes

Generally, pipes run horizontally through stud walls only in multiple-story homes. Rerouting a water pipe in a wall involves principles similar to those employed in rerouting wires. *Before rerouting pipes, remember to shut off the house water supply.* Also, be absolutely certain you are dealing with water pipes and not gas pipes.

For galvanized iron pipe, you need to rent a pipe cutter and a pipe threader the size of the existing pipe. Once the pipe is cut,

thread the ends and then connect it as shown with four 90-degree elbows and pipe lengths cut to fit. Because plumbing in walls usually serves an upper story, plumbing normally has to be run over the opening rather than under the house.

Copper pipe is rerouted in the same manner, but all the joints are soldered rather than threaded. If you haven't "sweated" copper pipe before, do all the preparatory work of drilling holes in the studs and cripples above the opening for the pipe to pass through, then have someone experienced do the soldering. (See Ortho's books, *Basic Home Repairs* or *Basic Plumbing Techniques,* for details on soldering copper pipe.)

If you run into gray or black plastic pipe from 1½ inches to 3 inches in diameter, you have found

**Rerouting electric cable and plumbing pipes**

Plumbing pipe through planned doorway

Electric cable through planned doorway

90° elbow · Rerouted cable · Steel nail protectors · Rerouted pipe

New outlets (one inside, one outside) where new cable joins old

a vent pipe. This material is relatively easy to work with. Cut the pipe with a crosscut saw above and below the opening, then connect the pieces with plastic elbows. The plastic glue used in making the connections is available where you buy the fittings. Coat both the pipe and the inside of the elbow with glue, then fit them together with a slight turning motion. Be sure to line up the fitting exactly as you turn it, because the glue sets up hard in about 10 seconds.

Wherever plastic pipe or copper pipe goes through a stud, cripple, or plate, put steel nail protectors, available at hardware stores, on each side of the stud, plate, or cripple where the pipe passes through. These prevent you from driving a wallboard or sheathing nail into the pipe.

Having dealt with these basic considerations, take a deep breath and prepare to gash that wall.

## Framing a Door Opening
### Platform-Style House

Before you cut the interior wall, try to locate the hinge side of the door against an existing stud. To locate studs, use a stud finder, which has a magnetic needle that is drawn to the nails holding the drywall to the studs. Or, since you must remove the baseboard along the wall, see if there isn't a little space between the drywall and the floor where you can see or probe a stud.

Once you have located that stud, use a level to find the vertical, then snap a chalkline from ceiling to floor along the inner edge of the stud. Now measure across the wall the width of the door unit, including jambs, plus about 1 foot, or to the nearest stud beyond the opening, to give yourself room to work. Snap a line down the center of the stud to mark the other side of the opening; working with the stud's center gives you room to nail on wallboard after the door is installed.

Whatever type of interior wall you have, make the cut with a carbide-tipped circular saw since you are likely to hit some nails. Set the blade just a little deeper than the

**Door opening in platform-style house**

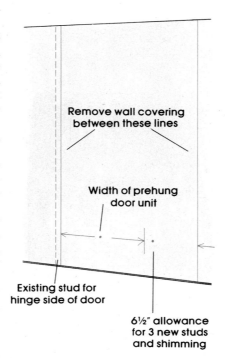

Remove wall covering between these lines

Width of prehung door unit

Existing stud for hinge side of door

6½" allowance for 3 new studs and shimming

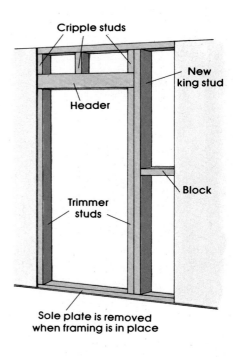

Cripple studs

New king stud

Header

Block

Trimmer studs

Sole plate is removed when framing is in place

thickness of the wall, which you can judge by checking behind the baseboard or punching a hole in the opening. Wear protective goggles, since a lot of small material will be flying about. Cut the wall covering along the chalklines from floor to ceiling. Remove the wall covering and pull out any insulation.

With the power saw, cut deeply into each stud that must be removed. If you cut close to their bottom edges, you can reuse them in framing the opening. Since a circular saw won't cut all the way through the stud, hook a hammer behind it at the cut and pull toward you to break it. Pry each 2 by 4 loose from the plates and the exterior wall nails. Bend the wall sheathing nails flat and cut the nails extending through the plates. Note that you do not need to cut through the exterior wall until the door opening is framed.

Use a level to check the plumb of the stud on the hinge side of your opening. Make that one a king stud. If it is slightly out of plumb,

hammer it over until it is right. However, if it is markedly out of plumb, remove it and put in a new one, since too much straightening may leave it loose and wobbly.

Once the king stud is ready, cut a trimmer stud 80 inches long and nail it to the king stud. Measure the width of the door unit, plus 2 inches to allow for shimming, then mark the positions of the other side's king and trimmer studs. Cut them both, nail them together, then toenail the unit in place to the plates. Cut and nail three blocks to fit between this unit and the nearest stud; nail the blocks to the plates and at the midpoint for additional stiffening. Nail the king and trimmer stud unit to the blocks. The blocks help keep this side from working loose after repeated slamming of the door.

Refer to the chart on page 8 for the proper header size, depending on the width of the opening. Check again that everything is plumb, then put the header in place and nail through the king studs. Cut cripple studs to fit above the header and toenail in place.

### Balloon-Style House

In balloon construction, the first step after both support systems are in place is to measure the rough opening height, which is 81½ inches from the subfloor. If you have a wood finish floor, subtract ¾ inch for the thickness of the floor and measure from there. The bottom of the header is located at this point above the floor.

See page 8 for the proper header size, then snap a chalkline across the studs to mark the bottom of the header and another to mark the top. Cut the studs along the top line, then cut them again about 12 inches up from the floor (why you do this is explained below).

Since you cannot install new king studs on either side of the opening, as you can in platform styles, you must use existing studs for king studs. That means you must use one or more extra trimmer studs

and possibly 1 by 4s on one or both sides of the opening under the header to narrow the rough opening down to the proper size, as illustrated.

In order to install these trimmer studs, you must pry out the fireblocks at floor level on the rough opening side of each king stud. Once this is done, measure the distance from the bottom of the header to the top of the joist or mudsill, depending on which side of the king stud you are working on (see illustration). Measure and cut these jack studs and nail to the king studs.

With the necessary number of jack studs in place, put the header up and nail it in place through the king studs. Toenail the bottom ends of the studs above the opening to the top of the header.

Once the rough opening is framed, remove the whaler, posts, and the temporary ceiling support.

### Framing a Window Opening

When installing a window opening, you must use the same support system as that used for a door opening. And since window openings can vary because of different-sized materials used in window frames, obtain the manufacturer's rough opening specifications from the dealer.

### Platform-Style House

Mark the rough dimensions of the window on the inside wall, then cut and remove the wall covering and insulation to the nearest stud beyond the marks. Choose a stud on either side as the king stud.

To find the proper window height, measure the distance from the floor to the bottom of a head jamb in an existing window. To that, add the thickness of the head jamb in the new window. This is where

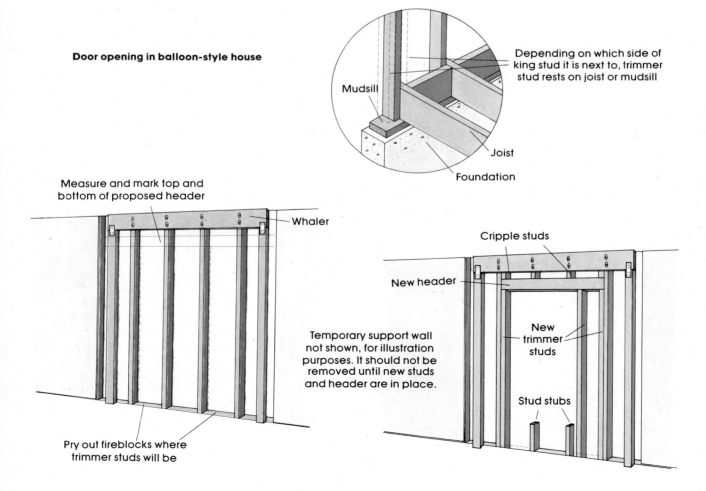

Door opening in balloon-style house

Depending on which side of king stud it is next to, trimmer stud rests on joist or mudsill

Mudsill

Joist

Foundation

Measure and mark top and bottom of proposed header

Whaler

Cripple studs

New header

Temporary support wall not shown, for illustration purposes. It should not be removed until new studs and header are in place.

New trimmer studs

Stud stubs

Pry out fireblocks where trimmer studs will be

the bottom of the header will be located. Add the width of the header to this (see page 8 for header sizes), and snap a chalkline across the studs. Mark the cutting lines on the studs, but don't cut yet.

Measure down the height of the new window unit plus ½ inch for shimming (or whatever the manufacturer calls for) and mark. This is where the top of the rough sill will be. If the window is more than 40 inches wide, use doubled 2 by 4s laid flat for the rough sill. Measure down the thickness of the rough sill and snap a chalkline across the studs. Cut there, then cut the studs at the top of the header marking. The stud ends at top and bottom become the cripple studs.

Measure the distance from the top of the sole plate to the bottom of the header. Cut a pair of trimmer studs to this measurement and nail one in place on each side. Measure and cut a rough sill and set it between the trimmers. With 16d nails, toenail its ends into the trimmers and face-nail it into the cripple studs. Install the header, toenailing it to the king studs (be careful not to drive the header out of alignment with the king studs) and trimmer studs. Add cripple studs above it, being sure to remember the ones that fit next to the king studs.

### Balloon-Style House

In balloon framing, remove the wall section from floor to ceiling, then install the support systems described on page 11. Build up the trimmer studs on both sides until you have narrowed the gap to the desired rough-opening size, just as you would for a door opening. Following the instructions for platform framing, install the rough sill, trimmer studs, and header.

## Cutting Through Exterior Walls

Cutting through the outside wall is somewhat exhilarating, because when that is done, you are ready to install the new door or window.

From inside, drill pilot holes at each corner of the rough opening. On the outside, connect these holes by snapping a chalkline, then cut

wood siding with a circular saw. Stucco, aluminum, and vinyl can be cut with either a carborundum blade or an old combination blade. (Opening a brick house, because of its complexity, is not covered in this book.) For a door opening, use a hand saw to cut the sole plate next to the trimmer studs on each side and remove it.

For a door opening in balloon framing, pry up the fireblocks between the stubbed-off studs in the opening. Cut the studs flush with the top of the joists. Cut a piece of ¾-inch plywood, which is the standard thickness of a subfloor, to cover the opening.

**Window opening in platform-style house**

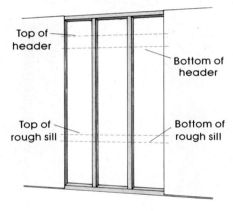

Top of header
Bottom of header
Top of rough sill
Bottom of rough sill

Temporary support wall not shown, for illustration purposes. It should not be removed until new studs and header are in place.

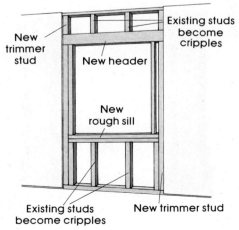

New trimmer stud
New header
New rough sill
Existing studs become cripples
Existing studs become cripples
New trimmer stud

## Altering an Existing Opening

In many cases of remodeling, you may want to install a new door or window that is either larger or smaller than the existing one. That means you have to change the size of the rough opening.

### Enlarging an Opening

To make a bigger opening for a door or window, you essentially have to remove the old rough opening and create a new, larger one in its place.

Remove the old door or window (pages 52–53) and the jamb material to expose the rough opening. If possible, leave one king stud and its trimmer stud intact, then remove the old header and cripples and the king and trimmer studs on the other side.

Cut the interior wall material back to the center of one stud beyond the planned opening, then build the new rough opening as described on pages 8–9 to fit around the new door or window. Be sure to check the size header needed for the new opening (consult the header chart on page 8); you may need a bigger one.

To put in a new window the same width as the old but longer, you only have to tear out and reframe the rough sill that supports it. Since this is much simpler than widening an opening, you may want to consider this method if you want larger windows.

### Decreasing an Opening

To shrink an opening, measure how much it must be diminished and then see if you can fit pieces of 2-by or 1-by material around the inside of the rough opening to bring it down to the smaller size. You can use 1-by or 2-by material in combination or even shingle shims to make the proper size reduction.

When you've installed the new door or window, cover the work with new wallboard, tape it, and cover the joint between window and wallboard with new trim. Outside the house, fill the gap with matching siding material and apply new trim.

# DOORS

This chapter details everything you need
to know about selecting and installing new doors,
whether you choose a prehung package
or hang the door yourself. Step-by-step
illustrated instructions include installation
of doorknobs and locks.

The doors on the exterior of your home serve several functions. Obviously, they open—to let in visitors, sunlight, fresh air, to let out the cat. And they close—to keep your family and possessions safe, to keep out rain and wind and snow, to keep in heated or cooled air. Interior doors provide privacy, conceal stored items, help you manage energy costs by closing off part of the house.

Whether exterior or interior, doors should compliment the look of your home. Their style may be sleekly modern, traditional, carefully handcrafted, inset with windows, or plain. Whatever it is, it should harmonize with the architecture and decor of the house. The pictures on pages 18-21 show some ways doors can enhance a home.

If you're building a new home or an addition to an existing house, you're already thinking about doors. If, instead, you're considering a remodeling job, take a look at your present doors. Do the exterior doors project the impression you'd like? Is the style appropriate to the house? Are they well kept up? How about the interior doors? Take a door inventory, looking for the doors that are warped, cracked, or sagging on their hinges. Doors should close securely, but not stick, and there should be

no gaps around the jambs. If you find damage that goes beyond routine repair (see pages 82-88), you may be in the market for new doors.

In choosing a door, there are a number of variables to take into account, in addition to style. Exterior doors are part of the weather seal of your home. Not only do they need to fit snugly and be properly weatherstripped, but any glass may need to be dual, for energy savings. As protection against crime and fire, you may want a metal door. On the other hand, you may prefer French or sliding glass doors, to open the house to the outside and bring in a beautiful view. Usually used at the back of the house, opening onto the patio or garden, these doors can flood a room with light. For a front door, you might choose a set of double doors, which signal a broad welcome to visitors.

Inside, you can choose from standard doors, pocket, bifold (often used for closets), or sliding closet doors. Perhaps you'd like the look, lighter weight, and increased ventilation of louvered doors. Mirrored sliding doors, installed like sliding glass doors, can add drama to a room, and give the impression that it is bigger as well.

Whatever type and style of door you select, you'll find instructions here for hanging it yourself. Pages 22-23 will help you choose the right one. Consult pages 6-9 to frame a door opening in new construction, or pages 10-15 if you are adding a doorway to an existing wall. Then proceed with the appropriate section of this chapter, beginning on page 24: hanging a prehung door, hanging a door from scratch, or installing sliding glass doors, a pocket door, bifold doors, or sliding closet doors. To complete a door installation, add a suitable knob and a lock, if necessary (see pages 38-39), and trim around the edges, as described on pages 40-41.

"Welcome to our home." Your front door says it for you. The formal symmetry of this Georgian entry with its topiary Texas privets makes an elegant statement. The solid wood door with brass plate and handle is topped by a fan window and flanked by beveled-glass panels. Lattice screens mounted on the inside provide privacy. With its pleasing proportions, the doorway extends a gracious welcome to the visitor.

# A GALLERY OF DOORS

The grace with which a front door performs its functions—securing its occupants and their possessions, yet making visitors feel welcome—is a combination of style and detail. Here, a variety of styles teams with the luster of polished brass, the sparkle of glass, and the visual appeal of contrasting finishes in an array of appealing doorways.

The pedimented entryway shown opposite makes an impressive introduction to a traditionally styled house. Its formal elegance includes classical columns and vertical window panels framing an oak door.

Classic simplicity distinguishes the Colonial-style door shown above, left. Part of its appeal lies in carefully chosen accessories: the gleaming brass of the knocker and kickplate, the balance of a pair of lantern sconces.

A broad old oak door (above, right) features an arched inset of small panes. Sheltered by a roofed overhang, it bids a warm welcome.

A casual charm marks the entry shown at right. Contrasting paint accents the panels of the wood door in a setting of variegated brick with potted plants and a pair of inquisitive geese.

An open door is an invitation. Here, a Dutch door and three sets of French doors encourage you to step over their thresholds and into the interiors beyond.

Clean-lined contemporary doors set between matching windows (opposite, top) form a wall of glass opening to a deck. When the doors are closed, the continuous horizontal lines of the muntins emphasize the breadth of the opening.

The classic Dutch door offers the security of closure combined with the convenience and appeal of the open door. The front-door version shown opposite, lower left, is solid below and glazed above. Made of poplar, it is crowned by a glass panel and framed by a carved and columned casing.

Traditional multipaned French doors (opposite, lower right) open into a formal dining room. Glass-inset doors provide privacy and a sense of closure without impeding sight lines. These have the unusual touch of clear-plastic handles.

Leaded-glass interior doors (right) open into the hallway from the breakfast room, where sunlight, Colonial furnishings, and maple trim combine to create a picture worthy of a Dutch master painter.

# TYPES OF DOORS

**Exterior Doors**

Front doors are commonly 1¾ inches thick, and not less than 80 inches high and 36 inches wide. Back doors are the same height—as are all doors—but sometimes narrower, down to 32 inches. Exterior doors should be solid-panel or solid-core, meaning the space between the front and back surfaces of the door is filled with either wood or particle board. A solid door offers more security, and it is less subject to warping brought on by humidity and different temperatures inside and outside. Exterior doors are usually single, double, sliding glass, French, or Dutch, depending on their location.

The construction of exterior doors is more complicated than it may first appear. A quality exterior door must not only be beautiful, but it must provide security, durability, and resistance to the elements. As you can see in the accompanying drawing, a well-made solid-panel door uses vertical-grain wood that is carefully fitted together with glue and dowels. The door consists primarily of the vertical stiles, the horizontal rails, and the solid filler material. Solid-core doors contain a particle-board filler; solid-panel doors are made entirely of wood. An exterior door may also include elaborate flashing, brickmold (exterior casing), and the sill.

Exterior doors may be flush, or they may have panels inset in the center section(s). Flush doors are made by covering the stiles and rails with thin sheets of plywood or veneer. Decorative molding may be attached to the surface. Some flush exterior doors—to be avoided—do not have a solid filler. Inset panels on exterior doors may be plain, carved, or glazed.

A third type of exterior door, the combination door, adds a storm door to provide extra insulation during winter months. During the summer months the glazing panels are removed and replaced with panels made of screening for improved air circulation.

**Door styles**

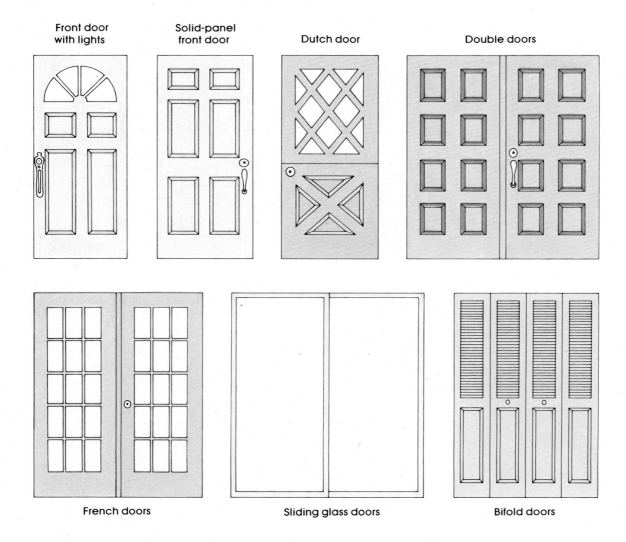

Front door with lights    Solid-panel front door    Dutch door    Double doors

French doors      Sliding glass doors      Bifold doors

Rapidly gaining in popularity are metal doors filled with insulating plastic. They are deterrents to both crime and fire. These metal doors are not a blank sheet of steel but are finished to appear very much like any good-quality door. They are normally sold in a prehung package.

## Interior Doors

Interior doors are usually hollow-core (meaning they contain only a lightweight filler), prehung units. Where soundproofing may be desired, such as for bathrooms or bedrooms, solid-core doors are preferable since they markedly reduce sound transmission. Common types are pocket, bifold, sliding, and mirrored sliding. A note of caution here about pocket doors: ideally they should be installed during the house construction phase. In remodeling, a section of wall covering the width of the door must be removed and the stud wall rebuilt to accommodate the door. Apart from the pocket door, however, installation of interior prehung doors is fairly simple, since no sill or flashing is needed.

## The Prehung Package

Both exterior and interior doors come in prehung packages. Such a unit includes the side jambs and the head jamb, and a door already mounted on hinges. The prehung unit needs only to be slipped into the rough door opening, shimmed until square, then nailed into place. With the exception of adding a sill and flashing for an exterior door, both interior and exterior prehung doors are installed in the same manner.

Prehung doors are usually slightly more expensive than building your own jambs and mounting your own hinges, but they can save hours of painstaking work. This section will cover both installation procedures, so you can choose your own level of punishment.

**Anatomy of a door**

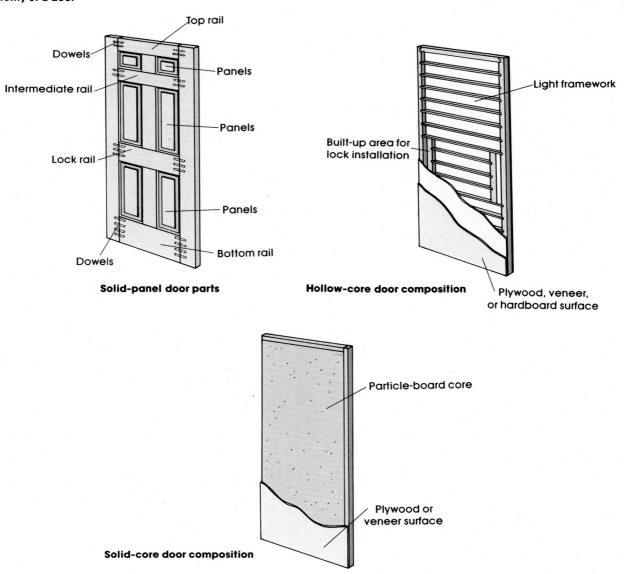

Dowels

Top rail

Panels

Intermediate rail

Panels

Lock rail

Panels

Dowels

Bottom rail

**Solid-panel door parts**

Light framework

Built-up area for lock installation

**Hollow-core door composition**

Plywood, veneer, or hardboard surface

Particle-board core

Plywood or veneer surface

**Solid-core door composition**

# PREHUNG DOOR

## Choosing the Door

Installing a door used to require the services of a skilled carpenter, but the prehung door has changed that. Now you just put it into place and nail. Well, almost.

Both interior and exterior prehung doors are installed in the same manner. However, a sill must be installed with exterior doors, and that is covered in the following section on hanging your own door.

The prehung door is factory assembled with the door hinged and mounted on the side jamb. A hole has been drilled for the doorknob. When selecting a door, you should know which way it will open and order either a "right-hand door" or a "left-hand door." This is always determined by the side on which the door handle is located when viewed from inside the room into which the door opens.

There are three basic styles of prehung doors. In one, the door is mounted inside the fully assembled jambs. In another, it is mounted to the hinge jamb only and you must nail together the head jamb and other side jamb included in the unit. In a third style, called a split jamb, tongue-and-groove jambs are fitted together from opposite sides of the rough opening. The door is already hung from one of the jambs. All these styles are installed in the same fashion.

## Installing the Door

Once placed in the rough opening, a prehung door must be shimmed to make it square since the opening itself may be slightly out of square. Using shingles as shims, place the first ones on both sides of the side jambs at the height of the top hinge. Measure the width of the jambs from outside to outside at the top of the door, then space the jambs this same distance at floor level and shim. Note from the illustration that shims are placed from both sides of the opening in an overlapping fashion. You control the spacing of the jambs by pushing the shims farther in or withdrawing them. On an

**Left-hand door** **Right-hand door**

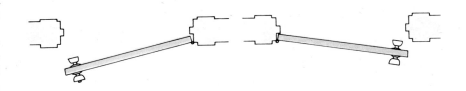

**Prehung door installation**

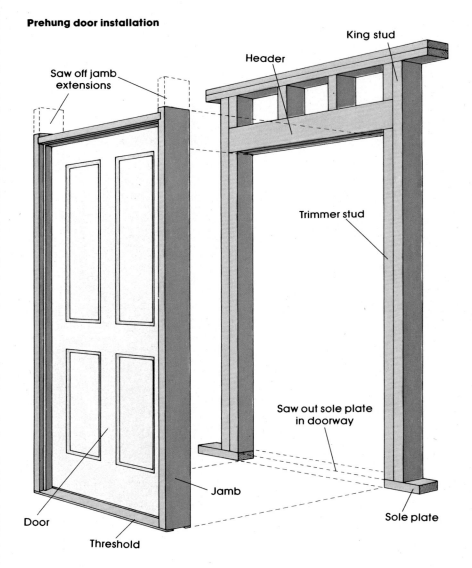

**Prehung door installation**

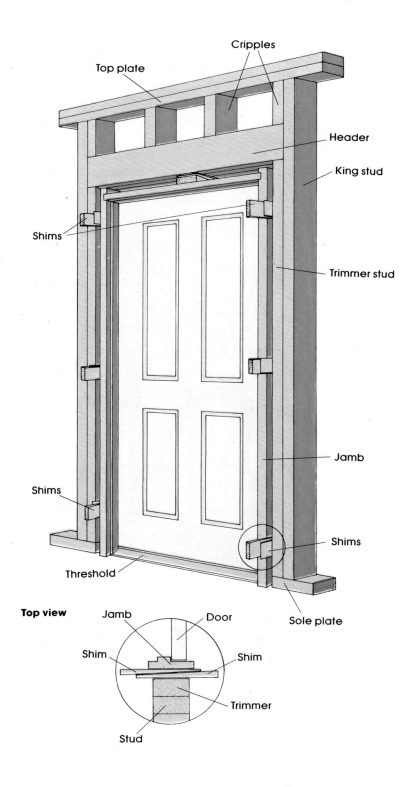

Cripples

Top plate

Header

King stud

Shims

Trimmer stud

Shims

Jamb

Shims

Threshold

Shims

**Top view**

Jamb    Door

Shim    Shim

Trimmer

Stud

Sole plate

exterior door you may not be able to slip a shim in from the outside because the brickmold (exterior casing) is in the way. In this case, cut the butts from several shingles, slip them in, then add the thin edge of another shim to wedge the first one in place. It is important to check that the head jamb is level. If it is not, shim under one side jamb until it is.

Center the jamb in the opening, then hold in place by driving a 12d casing nail through the shims into the trimmer stud near the top of the hinge-side jamb. Close the door, then place a steel framing square against the jamb corners to check that it is square. Adjust your shims until it is square, then nail the head jamb to the header.

Since the head jamb keeps the top of the unit rigid, the trick is to get the bottoms of the side jambs properly spaced. One professional trick is to drive a drywall screw nail through the jambs into the trimmer stud, then tighten or back off the screw nail until the jambs are exactly spaced. Put the shims in place and nail when everything is square.

When the door unit is centered and squared, nail the hinge side through the shims. Check again that the door swings freely, then nail the other jamb.

Now score the shingles deeply with a utility knife next to the jamb edge and snap them off.

Install the doorknob, striker plate, and a lock, if necessary, as described on pages 38–39.

If the door must be trimmed to clear carpeting, remove it from the jambs and cut it with a power saw as described on page 29. This should be done after the door is hung to get a precise clearance: it should just touch the top of the carpet.

The final step is to add the door casing that overlaps the edge of the jambs, the shims, and the edge of the drywall or paneling along the trimmer stud (see page 40–41 for installing trim).

# HANGING YOUR OWN DOOR

Hanging your own door allows for a more customized appearance. Most commonly, you would go to the trouble only for an exterior door; prehung units are usually adequate for interior doors. The instructions below are for an exterior door. Installing an interior door is the same except for the sill and the threshold, which are not needed. Exterior doors of homes always open to the inside, with the handle on the same side as the light switch.

To hang your own door, you will need a door, three butt hinges, sill material, a threshold, a door handle and deadbolt, side and head jambs, door stops, exterior and interior trim, and weatherstripping.

## Installing the Sill

In new construction or in cutting a new exterior door opening, you must install a door sill. It provides a finished appearance, and its downward slope sheds water that blows against the house.

Sills are made of hardwood and can be purchased at lumberyards. The sill should have a groove on the underside near the front to prevent water from running along the bottom edge toward the house. If it doesn't have one, cut a ¼-inch-deep groove with a circular saw.

In new construction the floor joists must be trimmed to accept the sill so that its back edge is flush with the finish floor. Another piece, the threshold, will cover the joint between the sill and the floor. When adding a new doorway to an existing house, you must cut away the flooring and subflooring to expose the joists. Make the cut directly under the inside edge of the closed door.

If the joists are running parallel to the sill, you must add a support member for the edge of the subflooring that was cut away and for the back of the sill. Do this by nailing two blocks, of the same dimensions as the joists, between joists on either side of the door opening. Cut two support joists to length and nail them through the blocks, as illustrated. One supports the flooring and the other catches the inner edge of the sill. Use a saw and chisel to notch the tops of the joists at the edge of the house. Make the notches 2 inches deep, then fit the sill into this trimmed area and check that it is level. Shim one end if necessary. Predrill the nail holes. When the sill is nailed in place, apply a bead of caulk under the sill where it meets the siding, then cover the joint with a length of quarter-round molding.

**Constructing a door jamb**

Rabbet

Head jamb

Rabbet

Side jamb

Side jamb

15°

Sill

Bevel inside and outside edges 15°

Drip groove

**Sill installation**

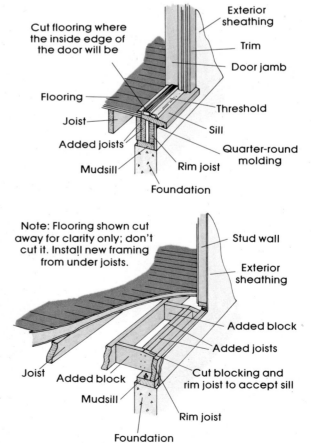

Cut flooring where the inside edge of the door will be

Exterior sheathing

Trim

Door jamb

Flooring

Threshold

Joist

Sill

Added joists

Quarter-round molding

Mudsill

Rim joist

Foundation

Note: Flooring shown cut away for clarity only; don't cut it. Install new framing from under joists.

Stud wall

Exterior sheathing

Added block

Added joists

Joist

Cut blocking and rim joist to accept sill

Added block

Mudsill

Rim joist

Foundation

## Installing the Jambs

It is easiest to buy material that is intended for door jambs; it will already be routed for the head jamb and cut to size. If you make your own, use stock that is at least a full 1 inch thick and rip it to the width of the house framing material plus the thicknesses of the exterior and interior sidings. At the top of the side jambs, rout a ½-inch-deep rabbet the thickness of the jamb material so the head jamb fits flush with the tops of the side jambs.

The rough door opening should be as wide as the door, plus the thickness of the two side jambs, plus ½ inch on each side for shimming.

Put the jambs together with glue and three 8d casing nails in each side.

Install the jambs in the opening with two shims behind each hinge location and two more equally spaced between. Check that the frame is plumb and square, then tack the top of the hinge side jamb in place.

Adjust the width of the jambs at the bottom to match that at the top by tightening or loosening a drywall screw nail driven through the jamb into the trimmer stud. Check again that the jamb is square by placing a steel framing square in the corners. Check that the head jamb is level; if it isn't, shim the bottom of one leg.

When everything is square, double-check that the door closes evenly. Nail the jambs to the trimmer studs through the shims. Use 12d casing nails with two at the top, two at the bottom, and six more evenly spaced between.

## Trimming the Door

The door should be trimmed to ¼ inch less than the jamb width to give a ⅛-inch clearance on each side. In addition, trim the door to allow for weatherstripping (see pages 78–79). Do all the trimming for width on the hinge stile so you won't have to deepen the lock mortise.

The last step is to bevel the inner edge of the lock stile ⅛ inch with a jack plane so it will clear the weatherstripping as it closes.

Allow ⅛-inch clearance at the top and bottom. The door will be cut to fit the threshold and weatherstripping after it is hung.

## Installing the Hinges

On doors up to 7 feet high, use three 4-inch butt hinges (or three decorative hinges). On doors over 7 feet high, use four hinges. The door and the jamb must be mortised so the hinges will be flush with the surface. Set the door on edge and brace it in the corner of a room, or use one of the door bucks illustrated to hold the door.

## Door Bucks

A door buck allows you to stand a door on edge while you plane it down to fit. Door bucks are simple to make and will save you the frustration of trying to hold a door with one hand while planing it with the other.

A simple buck can be made by using two bar clamps on the bottom of the door. Place one near each end with the bars extending in opposite directions. Place pieces of scrap wood between the jaws before tightening to protect the door.

Another commonly seen door buck is made by cutting a piece of ⅜-inch plywood 1½ inches wide and 12 inches long. Nail two pieces of 2 by 4 on edge near the center. Space them the width of the door plus ⅛ inch. Nail 2-by-4 legs at each end of the strip. When you put the door in the buck, the weight of the door will bend the strip down, causing the 2-by-4 blocks to clamp the door.

A third type is made from a block of 2 by 4 about 16 inches long. Cut a notch 1 inch deep and 2½ inches wide in the center of the block. Cut a wedge from the block, as shown, and use it to hold the door tight in the notch.

**Two kinds of door bucks**

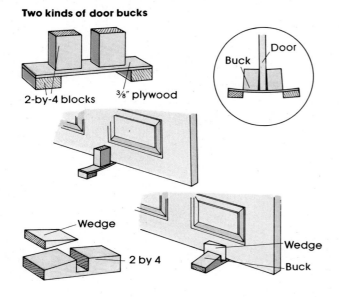

2-by-4 blocks    ⅜" plywood

Buck    Door

Wedge

2 by 4

Wedge

Buck

**Using door bucks**

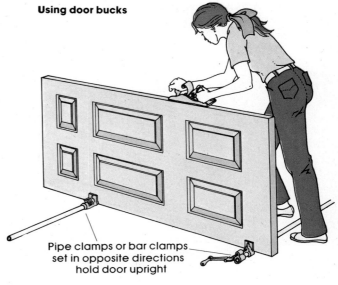

Pipe clamps or bar clamps set in opposite directions hold door upright

# HANGING YOUR OWN DOOR

## CONTINUED

Exact hinge locations vary according to taste, but one common practice is to place the top of the top hinge 7 inches from the top of the door and the bottom of the lower hinge 11 inches from the bottom of the door. Space the other hinge evenly between the top and bottom ones. Trace the hinge outline on the stile edge with a sharp pencil or knife. Allow the leaf to extend ¼ inch beyond the edge so the knuckle will not bind against the casing when the door is fully open. Remember the knuckle is inside, not outside, the house.

After the mortises are cut (see box), put the hinges in place and mark the center of each screw hole. Punch each mark with a nail before drilling to ensure that the drill bit does not slip off center. Be sure to drill straight holes, because if the screw goes in crooked, it will pull the hinge out of alignment.

With the door hinges installed, put the door in the jamb and mark where the hinges will fit, allowing the knuckle to extend ¼ inch beyond the edge. This is easier said than done, so arrange to have a helper. Put small shims under the door to raise it to ⅛ inch from the top. Mark the outline of the hinges with a sharp pencil or knife, then cut the mortises in the jamb just as you did the door.

A good trick in hanging a door is to mark and cut the top hinge first. Put the door up, screw the hinge to the jamb, then mark the other hinges and cut them.

If hinges do not line up, loosen the screws on both leaves. While a helper supports the door, tap the leaves together. Insert the pin and tighten the screws.

With the door up, check that it closes without binding anywhere. Ideally, the door has a ⅛-inch clearance on each side. For the perfect door, take it down and trim for a 3/16-inch clearance on the lock stile, using a sharp jack plane.

If the door sticks at the top of the jamb and the gap between door and jamb appears wider at the bottom, then you must shim the bottom hinge. Such unevenness is often caused by a jamb that is not plumb or a mortise cut too deep. Make a shim from the cardboard box the hinges came in. Cut it the height of the hinge and about ¼ inch wide. Loosen the hinge on the jamb and slip the shim behind the hinge. Retighten the screws.

Alternatively, the door may be binding at the top because that mortise was not cut deeply enough, so check your work before hanging that door.

## Mortising for Hinges

Hinge mortises can be cut with a router and template, a hinge marker, or the tried-and-true hammer and chisel. In all cases the hinge outline and depth must be marked on the wood with a sharp pencil or knife.

When using a router, the template is screwed in place to the door or jamb. Place the hinge against the door to mark the depth, then adjust the router bit to match. You will need a straight router bit and a ⅝-inch template guide bushing, which keeps the bit from striking the template.

A butt hinge marker speeds up your work by cutting all three edges at once. Just place it over the hinge outline and hammer it down to the hinge depth.

All this work can be done as well with a hammer and sharp chisel. Using a 1½-inch-wide chisel, score the top and bottom lines of the hinge outline. Hold the chisel at a 45-degree angle with the bevel up. Starting about ¼ inch away from the top line, make a series of cuts about ¼ inch apart and stop at least ¼ inch from the bottom line.

After making the cuts in the mortise area, hold the chisel vertically, bevel side in, and cut the back line of the mortise.

Remove the waste wood in the mortise by lightly driving the chisel from the edge toward the back line, bevel side up. The final step is to hold the chisel vertically and cleanly cut the top and bottom lines of the mortise.

**Cutting a mortise**

Door

Hinge mortise routing template

Chisel at 45° angle

Cuts ¼" apart

Bevel faces up

## Installing the Stops

The final step of hanging a door is installing the door stops, made of ½-inch by 1½-inch material. While you hold the door closed at the proper position, have a helper trace the outside edge of the door along the jamb with a sharp pencil. Measure and cut the stops to length. First nail on the head stop along the line, then the two legs. For greater security, stops for exterior doors can be milled as an integral part of the jamb so they cannot be pried off.

## Installing the Threshold

After the sill is installed and the door hung, remove the door. Install the threshold. If it is hardwood, drill holes and nail; if it is aluminum, use screws through the predrilled holes. Now measure the height of the threshold and cut the door to clear the threshold and any weatherstripping on it. Remember the threshold covers the gap between the sloping sill and the finish floor.

Measure the thickness of the threshold plus the weatherstripping, then remove that amount from the bottom of the door. Check the installation instructions for the weatherstripping on the threshold to see if they call for a bevel cut; many do, so the door edge will ride over it. If so, set the saw angle before making the cut. Use a circular saw with a fine-toothed blade, such as for cutting plywood. For a straight cut, use a fence made by clamping a straight-edged board to the door to guide the saw. Place pieces of scrap wood between the clamps and your work to protect the door.

## Finishing Touches

Finish the installation by adding the trim (see pages 40–41). You may want to paint the door, but you can also show off fine wood grain by applying stain and a clear finish. A double coat of oil-based sanding sealer will ensure a handsome appearance.

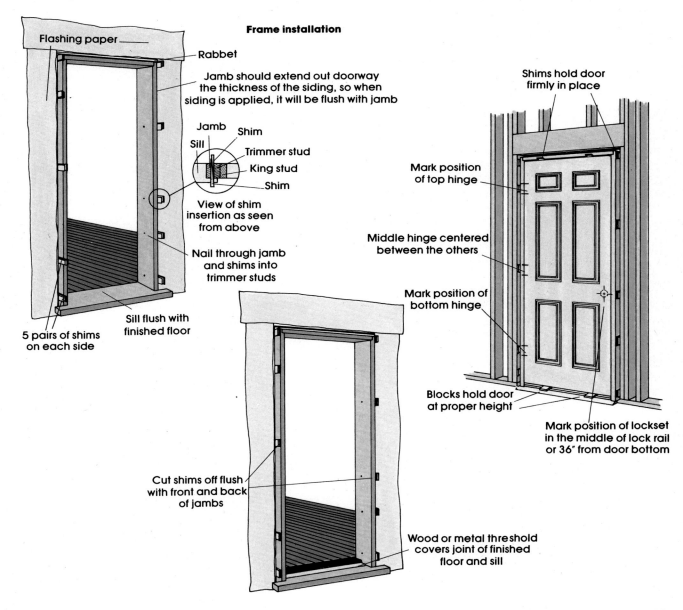

**Frame installation**

Flashing paper

Rabbet

Jamb should extend out doorway the thickness of the siding, so when siding is applied, it will be flush with jamb

Jamb
Shim
Sill
Trimmer stud
King stud
Shim

View of shim insertion as seen from above

Nail through jamb and shims into trimmer studs

Sill flush with finished floor

5 pairs of shims on each side

Cut shims off flush with front and back of jambs

Wood or metal threshold covers joint of finished floor and sill

Shims hold door firmly in place

Mark position of top hinge

Middle hinge centered between the others

Mark position of bottom hinge

Blocks hold door at proper height

Mark position of lockset in the middle of lock rail or 36" from door bottom

# DOUBLE DOORS

## Choosing the Door

Double doors are generally solid wood, sometimes glazed for additional light. They are available in many different styles in both wood and metal. You can buy just the doors, or order them prehung.

Both doors are hinged and both will open, but one (the one that includes the astragal, a wood strip that covers the crack between the doors) normally remains fixed. Sliding brass bars set into the edge of the door fit into brass fittings in the head jamb and the threshold to hold the door closed.

Double doors are installed essentially like a single door; the trick is to hang them straight and evenly. With prehung doors, where the jambs are precision cut and premortised, this is not difficult.

This section deals with installing prehung double doors. If hanging your own from scratch, read carefully the section on hanging your own door (pages 26–29).

## Installing the Jambs

The rough opening should be constructed in the same manner as for installing a standard exterior door, only wider. See the chart on page 8 for the proper header size. Cover the rough opening with flashing paper, asphalt-impregnated paper available in rolls at lumberyards, before installing the jambs.

If the prehung doors were delivered in the jambs, unscrew the hinge leaves on the jambs and remove the doors. Run three parallel beads of caulking across the floor of the opening, then set the jambs in the rough opening. Step on the sill to distribute the caulking as a weather seal.

Check that the sill is level; shim one end if necessary. Fit the brickmold, the exterior casing, tight against the edge of the rough opening. Square the jambs in the opening by placing a steel framing square in the corners, and use a level to check that it is true. Take special pains to ensure that the frame is absolutely plumb and square, and your doors should hang perfectly. Shim the jamb on both sides and above the header

jamb, then check again that all is plumb and level. Nail through the shims into the trimmer studs and the header. Nail the sill to the floor.

## Installing the Doors

Install the fixed door first. With a helper, put it in place as if the door were half open. Put some shims underneath the bottom of the door to support it. Screw the top hinge leaf to the jamb first. Use the longer screws that should have been shipped with the doors so the hinge is anchored securely through the jamb and into the trimmer stud. Screw the rest of the hinges into the premortised positions on the jamb.

Close the door and check the gap between the door and the jamb to see that the door is hanging straight. If not, you may have to shim out a hinge, but wait to do this until the other door is up.

Now hang the operating door in the same manner, using the longer screws in the top hinge leaf.

Close both doors and check the fit. If the doors are slightly askew, double-check that the hinges are firmly seated in the mortises. Minor adjustments can be made by shimming the hinges. See page 84 on how to shim a hinge. If the doors fit too tightly and must be planed down, remove the operating door hinges and plane the hinge edge.

After the doors are hung, install the doorknob and lock (see pages 38–39). To fit the door to any weatherseal threshold you might apply, see page 29 on removing and cutting the bottom edges of doors.

Finish the doors by installing trim around them (see pages 40–41). To protect the doors, apply a sanding sealer and stain or paint.

**Double door installation**

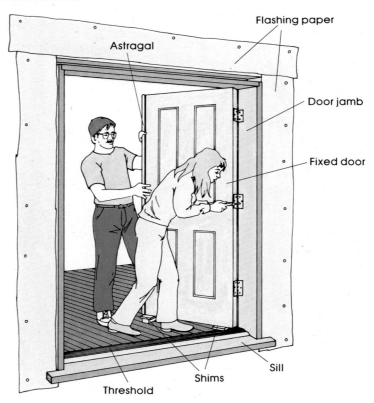

Flashing paper

Astragal

Door jamb

Fixed door

Sill

Shims

Threshold

# STORM & SCREEN DOORS

Exterior doors are not insulated, which allows cold to penetrate the house. In addition, unless the door is well weatherstripped, cold air will flow through cracks between the door and the jamb. The storm door provides protection by creating a dead-air space that inhibits the flow of cold air and the loss of heat. The storm door will also protect the finish on your door and help prevent moisture from penetrating it, which could cause it to swell and even warp.

Screen doors, which provide warm-weather protection against insects, are structurally the same as storm doors and installed in the same manner.

### Choosing the Door

Storm doors may be made of wood, in which case they are installed like a prehung door (see pages 24–25). The instructions that follow are for the more common aluminum-frame door. These instructions also apply to combination storm and screen doors, in which the upper glass panel can be replaced with a screen during summer months.

Before you purchase a storm door, measure the width of your door opening. A snug fit is necessary for the storm door to be effective. When shopping, compare the price of a purchased storm door with the cost of having one custom-made. The difference may not be that much, and a custom-made door will give you a tighter fit.

### Installing the Door

The storm door is fairly simple to install, but some cutting is often required. The door is shipped all assembled, with hinges in place. But in many cases the metal jambs have been left several inches longer than the door height so you can cut them to fit your door opening. Use a hacksaw to cut the jambs, cutting at an angle to match the slope of the door sill. To make the cuts, you may have to remove the adjustable door sweep at the bottom of the storm door.

Place the door in the opening and shim at each bottom corner until it is centered and square. Note how the Z-shaped flanges on the storm door jambs fit over the door trim. When the door is centered and square, drill pilot holes in the door trim through the flange holes; screw the flange to the trim.

Open the door and lower the door sweep until it makes contact with the door sill. Tighten the screws to hold it in place.

Following the manufacturer's instructions, install the door latch and the self-closing mechanism.

**Screen/storm door installation**

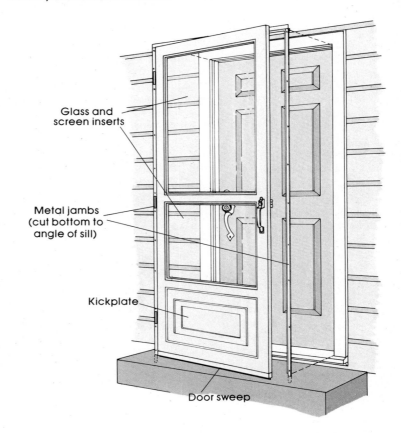

Glass and screen inserts

Metal jambs (cut bottom to angle of sill)

Kickplate

Door sweep

**Top view**

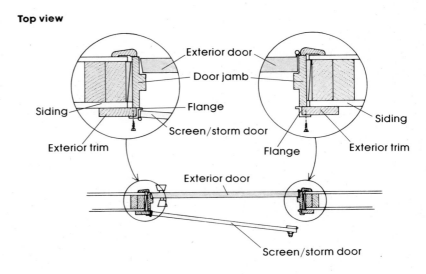

Exterior door
Door jamb
Flange
Siding
Screen/storm door
Exterior trim
Flange
Siding
Exterior trim
Exterior door
Screen/storm door

# SLIDING GLASS DOORS

## Choosing the Doors

For an instant transformation of a house, nothing succeeds quite like a sliding glass door. These doors are probably most widely used at the rear of a house. Although generally sold at standard 6-foot 8-inch heights and 6-foot to 8-foot widths, they can be ordered to custom-fit almost any need you have. By installing them yourself, as explained here, you will save considerable money.

Since you pay for quality, shop around carefully before you make a selection. For most windows, local codes require safety glazing. If you live in a cold climate, consider dual glass doors, or the heat loss through that expanse of glass will be extravagant.

Security is another consideration with glass doors. Glass is simply more vulnerable than metal or wood. You can, however, make it harder for a burglar to pry the door back and snap the lock. Choose doors with solid locks, and cut a length of dowel or 1 by 1 to fit between the edge of the sliding door and the wall so the door cannot be opened. Most doors are sold with a screw in the head jamb that just clears the door but prevents it from being pried up and out of the lower track. If your door doesn't have one, drill a hole through the head jamb into the header and install a screw.

Sliding doors usually have either wood or aluminum frames. If you choose aluminum, look for those with thermal-break frames, which prevent the aluminum from conducting cold into the house. Plan on putting the doors in a location that takes advantage of the low angle of winter sun; block the summer sun with roof overhang or outside blinds. Or look for doors made with narrow blinds placed between double panes.

Note that sliding doors can be arranged to open either to the right or to the left. After the frame is installed, put the fixed window in place first where you want it, then put the sliding door on the inside track on the opposite side.

## Installing the Doors

Have the doors on hand before you are to install them.

The rough opening should be ½ inch larger than the door unit on both sides and the top (or whatever the manufacturer specifies). Take special care to ensure that the trimmer studs are plumb and that the header is level. Minor variations can be corrected with the shims.

Since sliding glass doors are usually shipped with the jambs unassembled, the first job is to put them together, which is done simply with screws at the four corners. Before putting the frame in place, lay two thick beads of caulk along the floor near the edge of the opening to provide a weathertight seal.

From the outside, have someone help you place the frame in the opening and align it so there is an equal gap on each side. Step on the sill to distribute the sealant and to make it lie flat on the floor.

Check the sill with a level. If one side is lower, use several shims along that end to level it.

Nail the sill down with 8d galvanized nails spaced about 12 inches apart for aluminum-framed doors; use countersunk screws in wood-framed doors. Do not drive them all the way in until the rest of the frame is properly set.

Use a level to check that the

**Sliding glass door installation**

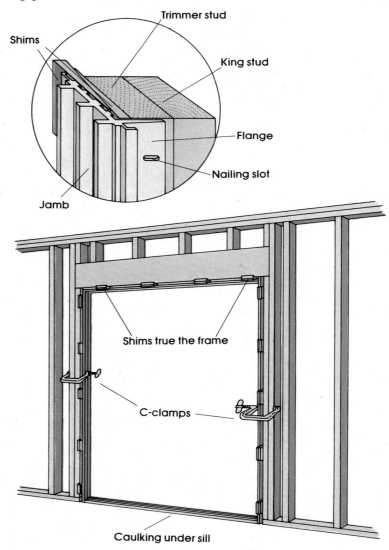

frame is true in the opening—not leaning in or out—and hold it in place with a C-clamp on each side. This will also draw the outside metal flanges or wood trim tight against the siding. Do not nail through the flanges or trim to the side of the house.

Next, place a straight board along each jamb to see if it bows in or out anywhere. Correct any distortions with shims.

Even if the jambs are straight, use five pairs of shims on each side to keep the frame solidly in place. Use four pairs along the head jamb. Use a steel framing square in each corner to check that the frame is square. Screw the metal frames to the rough opening through the predrilled holes in the jambs and head jamb; nail or screw wood frames to the trimmer studs with 12d casing nails through the shims.

Slip the head jamb flashing, which usually comes with the unit, under the siding above the door and fit it over the head jamb. Hold the flashing in place by nailing it through the siding; do not nail it to the head jamb.

In most cases the metal sill overhangs the opening and must be supported. Cut a length of wood about 1/8 inch narrower than the overhang, coat the top with a bead of caulking, and nail in place.

Next, put the stationary door in place in the outer channel on either side, depending on where you want the sliding door. On many makes of aluminum doors you will note that the top corner of the frame of the fixed door is partially cut through. The door will not fit into the top channel until you complete the cut with a hacksaw and remove that piece of metal.

The stationary door must fit tightly into the side jamb. If you can't push it in by hand, place a length of 2 by 4 against the door edge to protect it and rap on it to force the door against the jamb.

On wood doors, the rails are mortised to accept holding brackets. Put the brackets in place, drill into the head jamb and sill, and secure them with 1-inch number 8 screws. On some metal frames the door is secured to the frame from the inside with screws placed through predrilled holes.

Place the sliding door into the frame next. On wooden doors, first put the security screws into the head jambs, then remove the head stop. Position the bottom of the door first, with rollers resting on a rail in the sill, and then press the top firmly against the weatherstripping. Screw the head stop back in place.

On metal doors, first remove the security screw. Slip the top of the door into the head jamb channel first, then lift the door and set the rollers on their rail. Open the door and install the security screw in the head jamb.

Slide the door back and forth to check the movement, then close it. If one end of the door is lower than the other, causing a poor fit and a drag on the track, adjust the rollers at the bottom corners. In some cases the adjusting screw is on the edge of the door. In others, unscrew caps on the inside door corner and use a screwdriver to turn the recessed adjusting screws until you have a perfect fit.

When the doors have been satisfactorily adjusted, add the trim around them (see pages 40–41).

Finally, check that the latch closes properly. If it doesn't, turn the adjusting screw by the door latch until it catches firmly.

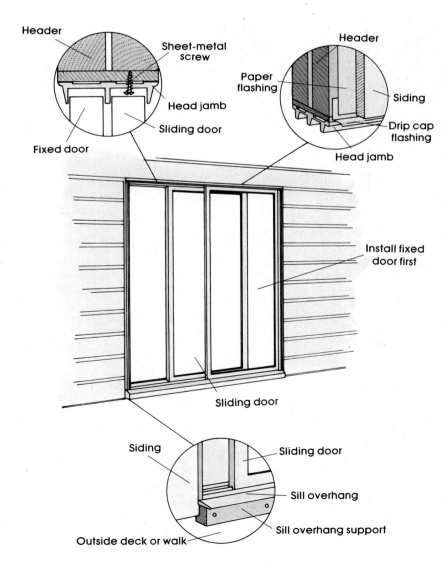

Header
Sheet-metal screw
Head jamb
Sliding door
Fixed door

Header
Paper flashing
Siding
Drip cap flashing
Head jamb

Install fixed door first

Sliding door

Siding
Sliding door
Sill overhang
Sill overhang support
Outside deck or walk

# POCKET DOOR

## Choosing the Door

The pocket door is commonly sold in one of two basic styles: a ready-made unit complete with the door, or just the hardware, to which you add the door of your choice.

The ready-made units are sold in a variety of standard door widths; they are all 80 inches high. Kits that supply just the hardware include adjustable overhead tracks, wheels that attach to the top of the door and fit in the track, a pair of split jambs and a pair of split studs. With this kit you can choose whatever type of door you want.

## Preparing the Opening

Regardless of what type of pocket door you plan to install, the first step when installing the unit in an existing wall is to remove the paneling or drywall. Determine where you want the door opening to be. Position the latch side of the door against an existing stud, if possible. From there, measure across the wall twice the width of the door opening. Find the nearest stud beyond that point, snap a chalkline down the center of the stud, and cut the wallboard along that line. Snap another chalkline on the wall over the center of the stud at the latch side of the door and cut the wallboard along the line. Take down the drywall and then remove the intervening studs by sawing and pulling them out. Cut near the top or bottom so you can reuse them in framing the door. If any nails remain, cut them flush to the plate using nippers or a hacksaw. If you are turning an existing doorway into a pocket door, remove the door framing material, including the header.

Using the framing methods for door openings described on page 8, install new trimmer studs and a new header. The bottom of the header should be about 1½ inches above the door to leave room for the track. Plumb and square the opening.

## Installing the Ready-Made Unit

The easiest type of pocket door to install is the ready-made unit. It is sold with a hollow-core door inside the frame slats and with the head

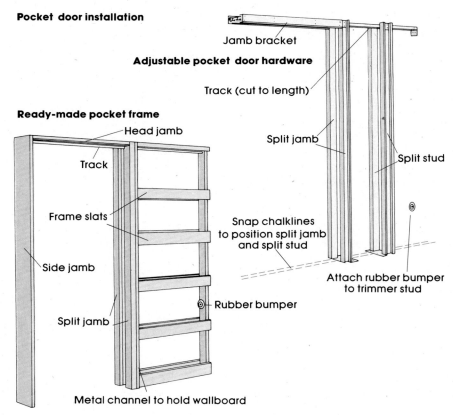

**Pocket door installation**

Jamb bracket

**Adjustable pocket door hardware**

Track (cut to length)

**Ready-made pocket frame**

Head jamb

Track

Split jamb

Split stud

Frame slats

Snap chalklines to position split jamb and split stud

Side jamb

Split jamb

Rubber bumper

Attach rubber bumper to trimmer stud

Metal channel to hold wallboard

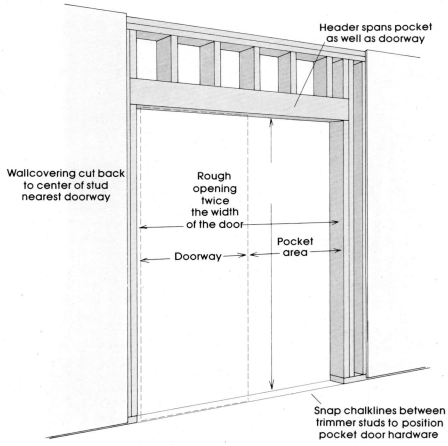

Header spans pocket as well as doorway

Wallcovering cut back to center of stud nearest doorway

Rough opening twice the width of the door

Doorway

Pocket area

Snap chalklines between trimmer studs to position pocket door hardware

jamb, side jamb, and overhead track taped to the slats. From the illustration you can see how it looks when the pieces are assembled.

When the opening is ready, remove the door, jambs, and track, and put the frame in the pocket. Check that it is plumb and level, then nail it to the trimmer stud.

Now mount the wheels on the top of the door about 1 inch from each end.

Put the side jamb in place against the trimmer stud on the latch side of the opening, then install the head jamb. Place shims between the head jamb and the header to both level it and stiffen it, then nail the head jamb through the shims to the header.

Screw the overhead track to the head jamb, being careful to keep the track centered. Lift the door and hook the wheels onto the track. Adjust the wheels until the door just clears the floor or carpet and hangs straight when closed.

Re-cover the studs with drywall or paneling, then cut and install trim around the door opening.

### Installing the Adjustable Unit
With this unit, the first step is to put the overhead track in the opening and open it until both ends are flush against the trimmer studs. Check that it is centered and level, then nail at each end to the trimmer studs.

Snap a chalkline on the floor between the outer edges of the trimmer studs at each end of the opening. These are guides for positioning the split jambs and studs in the pocket.

Place the split jamb at the edge of the door opening. Screw the top to the overhead track, then use a level to make sure it is plumb. Screw the bottom to the floor along the chalk lines. Repeat this step with the second split stud.

**Gliding Mechanism.** To hang the door, first place four factory-supplied screws in the top edge of the door. Locate them according to the instructions for your particular kit, usually two at each end. Now slip the door halfway into the pocket and put the wheel and gliding

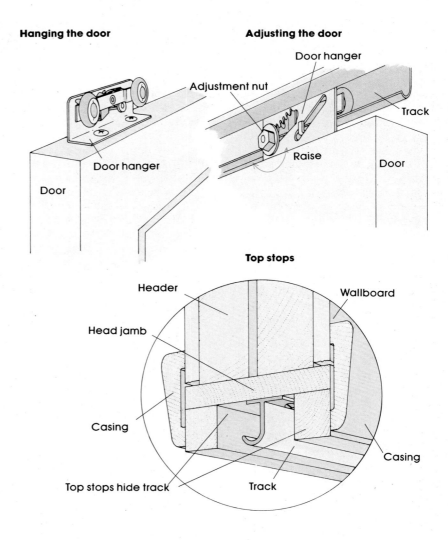

**Hanging the door**

Door hanger
Door

**Adjusting the door**

Door hanger
Adjustment nut
Track
Raise
Door

**Top stops**

Header
Head jamb
Wallboard
Casing
Casing
Top stops hide track
Track

mechanism into the overhead track. With a helper, raise the door and hook the brackets over the screws. Tighten the screws down. The door is now hung but must be adjusted to the proper height.

On each gliding mechanism is an adjusting screw that is turned by a wrench provided by the manufacturer. Turn the screws until the door is level and just clears the floor or carpet.

Next, the door guides are installed at the base of the split jamb, one on each side of the door. Screw them into the wood nailing strip and adjust until there is just ⅛ inch clearance from the door.

Install the rubber door bumper on the trimmer stud inside the pocket, at the midpoint of the stud. Push the door against the bumper. The

outer edge of the door should extend ⅜ inch beyond the split jamb. The bumper can be extended outwards by putting washers under it, or it can be trimmed with a knife.

Cover the opening around the door with drywall or paneling. Cut it flush with the edges of the split jamb and the overhead track. Nail it to the nailing strips on the jamb and track.

To cover the metal track, nail standard doorstop material (about ⅜ inch by ⅛ inch) through slots in the overhead track into the nailing strips and to the split jambs on both sides. Position the stops ⅛ inch from the door on both sides. Nail a length of jamb material to the trimmer stud on the latch side of the door.

Finally, trim the doorway with casing (see pages 40–41).

# BIFOLD DOORS

## Choosing the Doors

In places where a conventional door would simply be in the way, bifold doors come to the rescue. When open, they fit neatly against the door jambs; when closed, they provide a warm and interesting break in a wall. They are commonly louvered for minimum weight and ventilation, but may also be hollow-core. A big advantage is that they are quickly installed in an existing door frame.

Bifold doors come in different widths. A single unit consists of two doors hinged to each other. For larger openings, use two units that meet in the center.

You cannot always find doors to fit your opening exactly, but they can be trimmed down with a plane or table saw. When the doorway is too wide for your doors, trim the doorway with stock of a sufficient thickness to make the doors fit.

The hardware for bifold doors includes an overhead track that contains a top pivot, a bottom pivot, a slide guide, and an adjusting bolt at the bottom of the door to raise or lower it. If you already have the doors, you can buy just the hard-ware, or you can buy the doors and hardware as a kit.

## Installing the Doors

Measure the width of the door opening and then, if necessary, cut the overhead track to fit with a hacksaw. Place the track in the center of the head jamb and mark the center of the predrilled screw holes. Take the track down and drill the holes in the head jamb.

Next, insert the rubber bumper on the door-closing side of the track. For a pair of doors that close in the middle, slide the bumper to the center of the track to cushion the doors when they close. Slip the top pivot brackets on the end (both ends for a pair) of the track, then screw the track to the head jamb.

Push the top pivot bracket(s) against the doorway but don't tighten the holding screw yet. Drop a plumb bob from each end and position the bottom pivot bracket(s) directly under the top one(s). Screw them to the wall and to the floor, as shown. If carpeting is to be installed later, cut a strip of plywood to fit under each bottom bracket thick enough to raise it slightly above the carpet. If your doors and hardware were bought separately, drill into the bottom of the door and insert the vertical adjusting bolt; drill and insert the top pivot and slide guide in the top of the doors, as illustrated.

Attach the doors one at a time by first setting the bottom pivot into the bottom socket. Tilt the door toward the center of the opening and slide the top pivot bracket over to the center of the track. Tilt the door up until the top pivot slips into the socket. As you continue to push the door back to a vertical position, insert the sliding guide into the track. Push the door all the way back to the door jamb, check that it is vertical, and tighten the holding screws on the top and bottom brackets. Open the door and raise or lower it if necessary by turning the vertical adjusting bolt in the bottom of the door. Do the same with the other door.

Now install the trim around the door (see pages 40–41).

Close the doors and screw the metal door aligners in place about 8 inches up from the bottom, either at one side or in the middle for a pair of bifold doors.

**Bifold door installation**

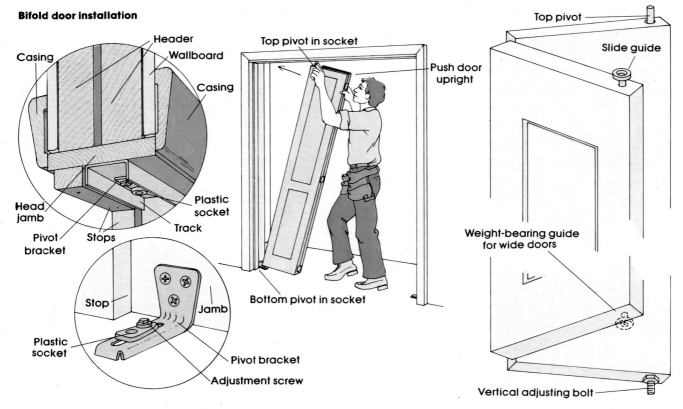

Casing · Header · Wallboard · Casing · Head jamb · Pivot bracket · Stops · Plastic socket · Track

Stop · Jamb · Plastic socket · Pivot bracket · Adjustment screw

Top pivot in socket · Push door upright · Bottom pivot in socket

Top pivot · Slide guide · Weight-bearing guide for wide doors · Vertical adjusting bolt

# SLIDING CLOSET DOORS

## Choosing the Doors

Sliding wood doors are commonly seen on closets because they are inexpensive and easy to install. You can use virtually any type of door, plain or louvered. Some models are mirrored, which can enhance the decor of the bedroom. These heavier doors are installed like sliding glass doors (see pages 32–33).

The basic hardware for sliding closet doors consists of an overhead track, a pair of wheels that attach to the top of each door, and door guides that are fastened to the floor. Better-quality hardware will also include a floor track with rollers built into it to smoothly guide the doors. The floor track is desirable; without it, the doors will tend to rattle. You can buy the hardware separately and use inexpensive hollow-core doors, or buy the doors and hardware in a kit.

The doors should be 1½ inches less in height than the opening. This allows 1¼ inches at the top for the track and ¼-inch clearance above the floor or carpet (this is not a critical measurement because the doors can be raised or lowered with adjusting screws on the wheels, as illustrated). However, each door should be ½ inch wider than half the opening so they overlap by 1 inch when closed. If you can't get doors of the proper width, trim the edges with a power saw guided by a fence (straight board clamped to the door) to narrow them, or add trim to the inside of the doorway to decrease the size of the opening.

## Installing the Doors

Most overhead tracks are adjustable. Place the track against the overhead jamb, open it until it touches both side jambs, then mark through the predrilled holes and drill the screw holes. Install the track with the channels to carry the wheels facing into the closet.

Mount a pair of wheels on the top edge of the doors about 2 inches in from each end of the door. With the overhead track up and the wheels mounted on the doors, hang the inside door on the inside channel first, then hang the outside door. Push the doors back against the door jambs and check how straight they hang by comparing them to the jambs; the framing process should have assured that the jambs are plumb. If a door is hanging crookedly, loosen the adjusting screw on the roller from the back (see detail) and raise or lower one end of the door until it hangs straight.

If your hardware includes track guides, remove the doors and place the guide track in the center of the opening. Replace the doors, center the track under them, and raise or lower the doors with the adjusting screw until they ride on the rollers. Remove the doors, screw the track to the floor, and replace the doors.

If your hardware does not include a track with rollers for the door bottoms, you can help keep the doors from swinging and banging into each other by the use of a metal or plastic floor guide. Screw the guide to the floor between the doors in the center of the opening where they meet. If the guide is adjustable, as they usually are, move the side pieces until there is ⅛ inch clearance from the doors.

Finally, install the trim around the doors (see pages 40–41).

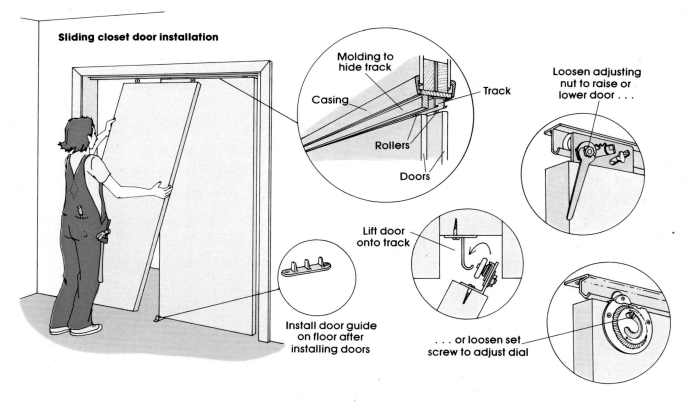

**Sliding closet door installation**

Molding to hide track

Casing

Track

Rollers

Doors

Loosen adjusting nut to raise or lower door . . .

Lift door onto track

Install door guide on floor after installing doors

. . . or loosen set screw to adjust dial

# DOORKNOBS & LOCKS

A visit to a hardware store or specialty door store will give you an idea of the wide variety of locks, doorknobs, and door latches available, including standard round metal knobs, glass or porcelain knobs, simple rim locks, and hardened-steel deadbolts. If security is a big concern, you may want to ask a salesperson which locks are recommended. In general, cylinder locks provide the least security. A rim lock is proof against most tampering, but some cylinders are more pick-proof than others.

The installation procedures for the different styles are essentially the same. Door hardware comes with installation instructions, but often these are somewhat incomplete. The instructions that follow give the basics of doorknob and lock installation.

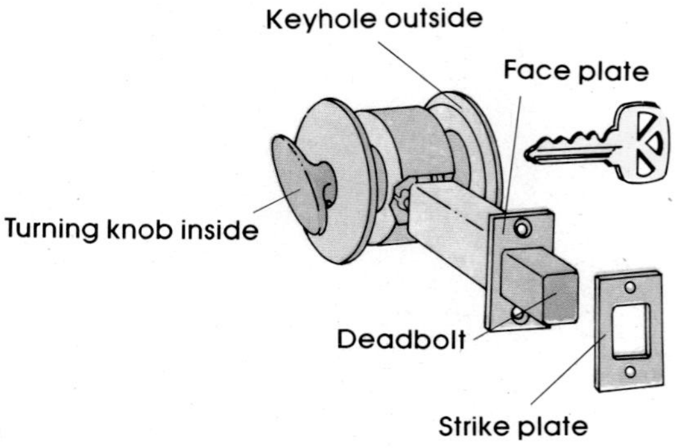

## Some Free Advice

For protection against break-ins, some locks are opened from the inside with a key rather than a knob; an intruder may break a window to get access to the lock but cannot open it without the key. However, fire officials frown on these locks, and in some localities they are illegal. Trying to find a key in the middle of the night when the house is burning can cause fatal delays.

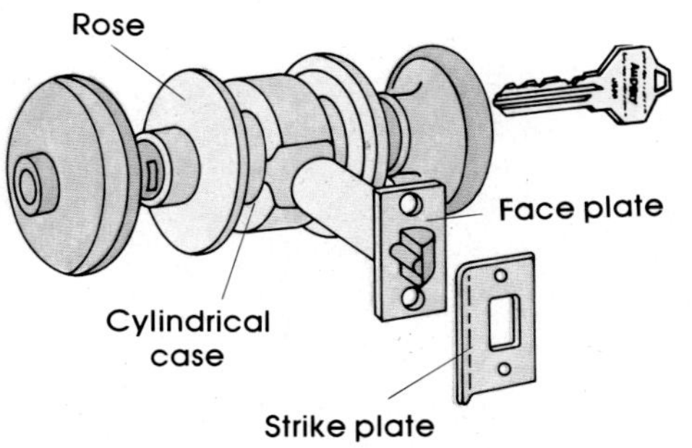

Whatever kind of lock you have, you should work out ways of exiting the house in the event of a fire, and practice these routes with the family. Make sure houseguests understand about key-operated locks and fire escape routes.

## Installing a Cylinder Lock

The cylinder lock is made in several different styles. Those with twist or button locks on the inside are used for bedrooms and bathrooms. Those with key locks are usually found on exterior doors.

The standard cylinder lock consists of two handles, two roses to cover the hole in the door, a central cylinder to retract the bolt, the bolt mechanism, the strike plate, and the face plate. Cylinder locks are always installed after the door is hung. In most prehung doors, the doorknob and bolt holes are already drilled. If you need to drill the holes, you will find with the doorknob set a cardboard template that instructs you where to drill and what size bits to use.

In measuring the holes, remember always to work from the "high side" of the door, the edge away from the stop.

The knob should be located the same height as other knobs in the house, which is usually 36 inches from the floor. Mark that position on the door, then use a square to draw a line across the face and edge of

**Cylinder lock**

Rose

Cylindrical case

Face plate

Strike plate

**Mortise lock**

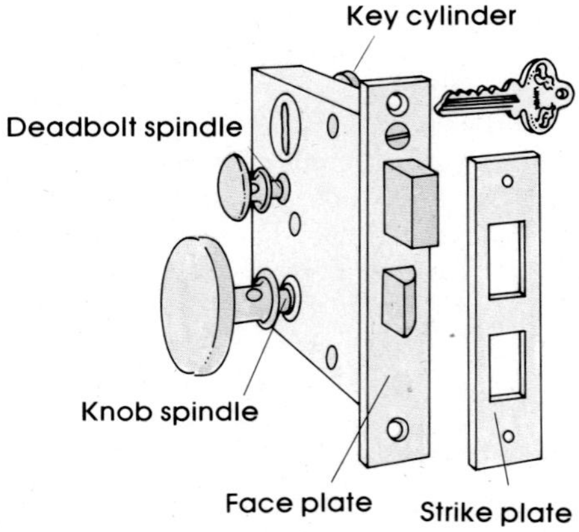

Key cylinder

Deadbolt spindle

Knob spindle

Face plate

Strike plate

**Rim lock**

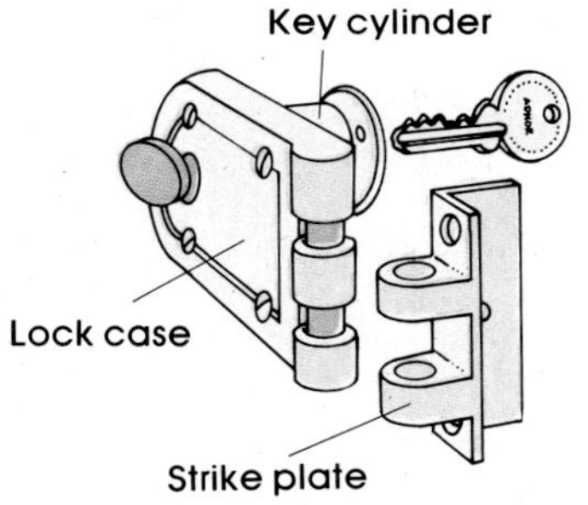

Key cylinder

Lock case

Strike plate

**Deadbolt lock**

Keyhole outside

Face plate

Turning knob inside

Deadbolt

Strike plate

the door. The holes will be centered on these lines.

Measure the thickness of the door. Interior doors are normally 1⅜ inches thick; exterior ones are usually 1¾ inches thick. The template shows you where to drill depending on the door's thickness.

To hold the door in place while you work, open it and drive a wedge under it.

Fold the template on the dotted lines and fit it to the door at the proper height. Use a nail or an awl to mark the center of the holes on the door face and edge.

The face of the door should be drilled with a hole saw for neat work. The required diameter is stated on the template; it is usually 2⅛ inches.

To prevent splintering, drill only halfway through the door with the hole saw. When the drill bit emerges on the other side, use that as a guide to complete the job from the other side.

Double-check that the mark for the bolt hole is centered over the cylinder hole, since sometimes the template slips while you are marking. Drill the bolt hole with a spade bit of the size specified on the template, usually either 1 inch or 15/16 inch. This hole must be perfectly horizontal and straight.

Locate the strike plate and face plate positions next. Close the door, slip a short pencil through the bolt hole, and outline its diameter on the door jamb. Open the door and drill a hole there about ½ inch deep to provide room for the bolt when closed. Make the hole slightly larger than the bolt diameter. Place the strike plate over the hole and outline it. Then put the face plate against the door over the bolt hole and mark its position.

The areas outlined for the two plates must be mortised so the plates are flush (see page 28). Screw the strike plate into position.

Next, slip the bolt into the door and fit the face plate over it. Slide the roses onto the knobs and fit the spindle through the bolt. Screw the two knobs together through the holes in the roses. If the bolt does not close completely, the strike plate is

not properly aligned or, more likely, you did not make the hole behind the strike plate deep enough for the bolt. Adjust the plate's position, or deepen the hole.

## Installing a Deadbolt

A deadbolt assembly requires a key on the outside and either a key or a turning knob on the inside. The deadbolt is a shaft of hardened steel that, when turned, enters a hole drilled through the door jamb and into the trimmer stud behind it for greater security. Follow the instructions for installing cylinder locks, since deadbolts are installed in essentially the same manner. The manufacturer's template will specify the size and depth of the hole into the trimmer stud. Place the deadbolt above the doorknob.

If the deadbolt does not shoot home completely, check that it is not hitting the strike plate, and that the hole is deep enough.

## Installing a Mortise Lock

These locks, mounted in a thin steel case, must be set in doors at least 1⅜ inches thick. In addition, they are set more deeply into the door than cylinder locks. If you have a glass panel in your door, measure from the door edge to the glass to make sure there is enough room to set the lock in the door. Shattering a door window while drilling the lock mortise almost guarantees cardiac arrest. Check the clearance also if you have an inset wood panel.

Mortise locks generally include a deadbolt in addition to the latch, which offers good security in one package. However, they are more time-consuming to install than cylinder locks, because a mortise, or square opening, must be chiseled into the door edge.

The first step is to mark the outline of the case centered on the door edge, 36 inches from the floor. Drill a series of holes within the outline. The drill bit should be 1/16 inch wider than the lock case. To remove the wood between the boreholes and to clean up the back of the mortise, use a special tool called a lock mortise chisel. To make the sidewalls neat, use a

standard wood chisel with the beveled side in.

Insert the lock and put the face plate over it. Mark the outline of the face plate and mortise the door edge so the face plate is flush with the door edge.

Now position the template that came with the lock, and drill the holes for the lock and knob. Use the drill sizes recommended on the template.

When you have assembled the lock in the door, coat the ends of the bolt and latch with chalk. Close the door, and turn the handle and lock to mark their positions on the jamb. Drill holes to accept the latch and bolt, then mark and mortise the jamb so the strike plate is flush on it.

**Mortise lock installation**

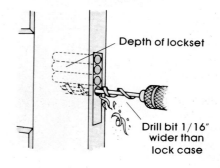

Depth of lockset

Drill bit 1/16" wider than lock case

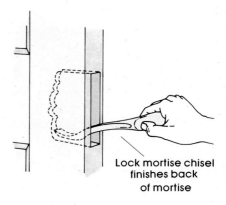

Lock mortise chisel finishes back of mortise

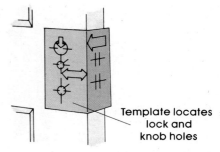

Template locates lock and knob holes

# DOOR & WINDOW TRIM

The functional job of door and window trim is to cover the gap between the wallboard or exterior covering and the door or window jamb.

Trim goes under several names: around an exterior door it is called brickmold; around interior doors and windows, it is called casing; around the outside of doors and windows it is called exterior trim.

The most finished appearance for interior trim is achieved by joining the side casing and head casing in a mitered 45-degree angle cut. If the casing is molded, then you should use a coping saw (see box) for a tight fit. Another method, which gives a somewhat rough-hewn appearance but is simpler, is to use butt joints between the head and side casings.

After the casing has been installed, use a nail set to drive the head of each casing nail below the wood surface, then fill the holes with wood putty. Paint, stain, or seal the trim to harmonize with your home's exterior.

### Assembling with Mitered Joints

Ideally, the casing should be set back from the inner edges of the jamb by 3/16 inch and not more than 1/4 inch. You can put a guide line along the casing edge by adjusting your square so that 3/16 inch protrudes, then sliding the square along the jamb with a pencil tip following the end of the blade.

Once the jamb is marked, cut the base of one side casing at a 90-degree angle. Place the trim along the guide line on the jamb. Mark the casing where the lines on the side and head casings meet. From that point, make a 45-degree angle cut on the casing. For precise work, you must use a miter and backsaw or power miter saw.

After nailing the side casing in place, make a 45-degree cut on one end of the head casing and fit it to the side casing. Mark the other end where the guide lines on the jambs meet and cut that 45-degree

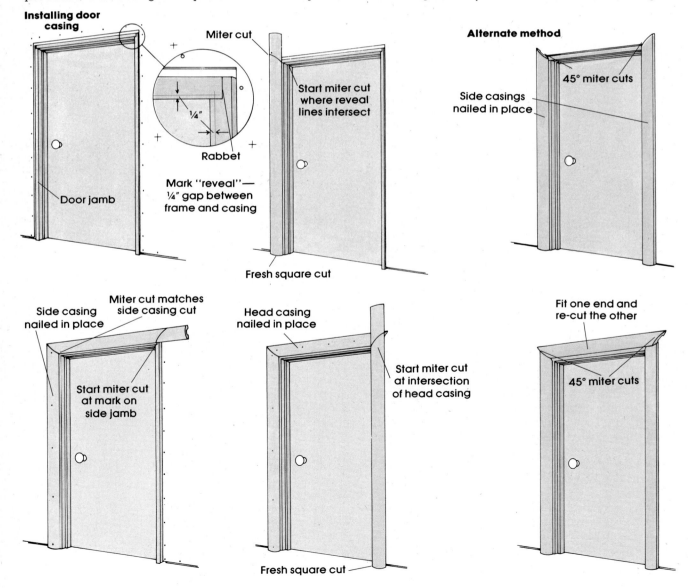

**Installing door casing**

Miter cut

Start miter cut where reveal lines intersect

¼"

Rabbet

Door jamb

Mark "reveal"—¼" gap between frame and casing

Fresh square cut

**Alternate method**

45° miter cuts

Side casings nailed in place

Side casing nailed in place

Miter cut matches side casing cut

Start miter cut at mark on side jamb

Head casing nailed in place

Start miter cut at intersection of head casing

Fresh square cut

Fit one end and re-cut the other

45° miter cuts

angle. Nail up the head casing.

Finally, cut the bottom end of the other side casing at a 90-degree angle and put it in place. Mark where it meets the head casing, then cut it and nail in place.

**An Alternate Method.** The above description is the textbook manner of putting up trim where the door or window is square. Unfortunately, they often aren't. As a result, the 45-degree cuts will not match up. Some pros do the job in the following way.

Mark the edge of the jamb 3/16 inch back, as described above. Cut the bottoms of the two side casings square and fit them against the jamb. Note where the top ends meet the right angle of the guide lines on the head jamb. Mark the side casings at these points and cut a 45-degree angle in each one. Nail them in place.

Next, take a length of trim for the head casing that is 4 inches longer on each side than the outer edges of the side casings. Cut 45-degree angles at both ends of this head casing. Now, fit the left end of the head casing to the left side casing and position it precisely on the guide line. Let the other end

overlap the casing on the other side. Check how the joint fits. If there is a gap, and all casing is right on the guide lines, then that side of the door is out of square. Check the other side in the same manner. If one side fits, put it in place, then mark the head casing's top and bottom edges to match the miter cut on the other side casing. Adjust your miter saw by this slight degree change and cut—*but* (an important but) cut the head casing 1/16 inch long and wedge it into position and nail. This helps ensure a tight fit. If a small gap still exists, it can be closed by lock nailing (see box).

## Assembling with Butt Joints

Installing casing with butt joints simplifies the job and is still handsome. The trim can be made more attractive by using a head casing larger than the side casing. As an example, if you use 1 by 3 stock for the side casing, use a 2 by 6 for the head casing. Use a router or a wood rasp to round off the outer edges of the head casing for a more finished appearance. You can also let the ends of the head casing extend beyond the sides by ½ inch to 1½ inches.

Before cutting the tops of the side casings, check that the head jamb is level. If it slopes slightly, adjust the cuts at the tops of the side casings. Use a long level to mark the cuts, then cut the head casing, put it in place, and nail.

## Trimming a Window

In addition to head and side casings, window trim includes a stool and an apron. The stool is installed first. It should be of quality wood such as clear pine or fir. If the stud wall is constructed of 2 by 4s, use 1 by 6 material; with 2 by 6 studs, use 1 by 8 material.

Notch the stool so that it covers the rough window sill and extends out on each side the width of the casing (which you will install next) plus about 1 inch. Nail the stool in place.

Rip the casing pieces so the outer edges are flush with the drywall. Following the instructions given above, install the two side pieces first, then the head casing.

The apron, commonly a 1 by 4, is nailed under the stool. The ends should be in line with the outer edges of the casings. Nail it in place after the casing is installed.

---

## Corner Techniques

**Lock Nailing.** When a mitered joint is slightly off, you can probably close the gap by lock nailing that joint. Do this by first squeezing some glue in the crack, then driving one casing nail through the head casing into the side one, and another nail from the side casing into the head casing, as shown. Wipe away excess glue immediately and sand lightly when dry. The trim wood is flexible enough that lock nailing will often close a gap in a mitered joint.

**Coping a Mitered Joint.** When working with molded casing, some of which is quite thick and elaborate, the joints must always be mitered so the molding will stay in a consistent line. But for a tight joint in this case, the back of one mitered piece must be "coped," so called because it is done with a coping saw. Turn the casing over and use the coping saw to cut a thin scallop of wood from the back. Coping is necessary only on one side of a mitered joint.

**Lock-nailed joint**

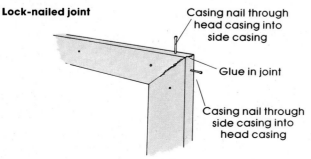

Casing nail through head casing into side casing

Glue in joint

Casing nail through side casing into head casing

**Coping the back edge of a miter joint**

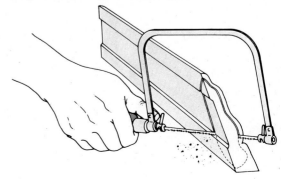

# WINDOWS

Here are step-by-step instructions to guide you in
selecting and installing all kinds
of windows, including special sections on
skylights and bay windows.

Windows function primarily to admit light and views of the outdoors. But a window has style as well as function, and its style should compliment that of the house. The photographs on pages 44–49 display some of the ways windows can enhance a home. You'll want to think about both function and style as you decide what kind of window you'll use.

What type of window you choose is largely a matter of personal taste, since one is not inherently better than others. Windows are basically either fixed or openable (see page 50 for illustrations).

A fixed window does not open to permit ventilation or cleaning, but its sealed edges provide excellent protection against air infiltration. You can install a fixed window in almost any shape and size, but if you choose a large size, it should be made of dual glass for energy savings.

Openable windows include casement, double-hung, single-hung, sliding, awning or hopper, rotating, and jalousie. Casement windows usually open outward but can be ordered to open inward. They provide excellent ventilation, and newer models open wide enough to permit cleaning the exterior from inside. Double-hung and single-hung differ in that both sashes of a double-hung open, while only one sash of a single-hung does. They provide less ventilation than a casement because only half the window can be open at one time. Older windows with weight-and-pulley systems tend to stick or rattle; newer ones with spring tension devices work well. These windows can be difficult to clean unless you get one with a removable or tilt-in sash. Aluminum-framed sliding windows are among the least expensive. As with

the double-hung, only half the window can be open at one time. The inner sash can be removed to permit easy cleaning of both sashes. Awning or hopper windows can be hinged at top or bottom and can open either in or out. Their construction creates good air flow and makes it easy to clean the exterior. The rotating window can open partially or rotate 360 degrees on its central axis, which makes cleaning easy. It is available in a double-pane version with a mini-blind built in for light control. Jalousie windows, with many small panes of glass, give good ventilation but cannot be well sealed for thermal control and are tedious to clean. They are most suitable for porches and warm-weather homes.

In this chapter, you'll find instructions on removing existing windows on pages 52–53, followed by directions for installing fixed-pane, wood-framed, metal-framed, and greenhouse windows, skylights, and bay windows. If you're doing new construction, see pages 6–9 for basic information on framing a window opening before you embark on installing the windows.

Another step to take before you begin window installation is to check the applicable building code requirements. All construction practices are governed by building codes, which are designed to ensure the structural safety of any building. Most city, town, and county governments adhere to one of the major model building codes, but some local codes are even more stringent for reasons particular to that area. Before doing any new construction, check with your local building inspector.

You will need a permit if any of your work involves structural changes, such as making a new window opening or altering the size of an existing one. If you replace a window with another the same size, you may not need a permit, but double-check with your inspector. When new electrical wiring is installed, or existing wiring is re-routed, a permit will be required. The same is true with any plumbing changes. For new construction, there are both minimums and maximums for the total window area, as well as requirements for openable windows and dual glazing.

To obtain a permit, draw up and submit specific plans on your project. They don't need to be fancy—you can do them on sheets of typing paper—but they need to include all pertinent information, such as the size of the opening, the size of the header, the size of the window, and the type of glazing.

The major consideration in designing this dining room window was to provide a clear view of the tree and the bay beyond. However, because the house is surrounded by predominantly traditional homes, the architect did not want to install a modern picture window. The compromise solution: a basically square opening that is modified by a graceful internal arch and crossbar. Anodized-bronze aluminum frames define the individual panes. The overall effect is one of softness with variety.

# THE GLASS MENAGERIE

Like the dining area on the following pages, the bedroom above is in the house pictured on the front and back covers. The dominant feature of the room—a magnificent arched window that admits a panoramic view of ocean and sky—nestles within the line of the unusual vaulted ceiling. The architect has melded contemporary style—large areas of glass—with traditional by setting the glass in rectilinear framing that echoes the muntins of the double-hung windows elsewhere in the house.

When the owners of the house shown opposite remodeled, one major goal was to let in more light. The addition of a second story allowed them to create the gabled window above the bed alcove. Custom-ordered to match the existing lower window in both size and style, the new opening has a distinctive peaked top that repeats the line of the exposed beams. The cutout in the new vertical wall acts as an interior frame for the new window.

# THE GLASS MENAGERIE

CONTINUED

The sun-drenched dining area on the preceding pages displays the magic that windows perform. Instead of picture windows, the architect has used a traditional window style more in keeping with the shingle-clad exterior of this country house. Opening onto an oceanside lot of dunes and grass, the floor-to-ceiling, wall-to-wall bank of double-hung windows fills the room with light. The room-opening effect is enhanced by filmy white curtains, white-painted woodwork, and the reflective surfaces of the tabletop and glazed-tile floor.

There are windows galore in the house shown above. Tempered ground-floor panels (all standard sizes) alternate with fir-framed doors; both are topped with rectangular fixed-pane windows. Contrasting squares of varying sizes pierce the upper facade. Concentrating the fenestration on the courtyard walls for privacy results in unrestricted view lines that connect the various living spaces. As shown in the interior view on page 4, 1-by-4 rough cedar siding covers both interior and exterior walls; it maximizes the continuity of space and light by minimizing distractions. At dusk, the interior lights give the home a warm, welcoming glow; in the day, exterior light floods the rooms.

Two views of an intricately designed house are shown above and at right. Set on a curving waterfront site, the seemingly separate structures are actually the two halves of a single home, joined by a glass atrium. The front of the house, at right, plainly shows how much one side is set back from the other. The design of this house is a carefully calculated interplay of repetition and variation. The width of the opening for the four windows at right matches that of the garage door; their simple square shape is repeated in the single window on the front of the other half and again in the upper-left panel on the back of the house, shown above. There, a new set of elements is introduced: unarticulated squares flanked by vertical panels. At the same time, the ground-floor bump-out and the inset above create a protected second-story deck. The windows are integral to all of these design considerations, providing both variety and continuity—and ample views of the lakefront setting in the bargain.

# CHOOSING THE RIGHT WINDOW

Once you have decided you need new windows, whether you are remodeling or have new construction, the big problem is deciding what type you want. Consult the charts and illustrations on these pages to understand key aspects of different kinds of windows, including both their good qualities and their limitations.

## Window Types

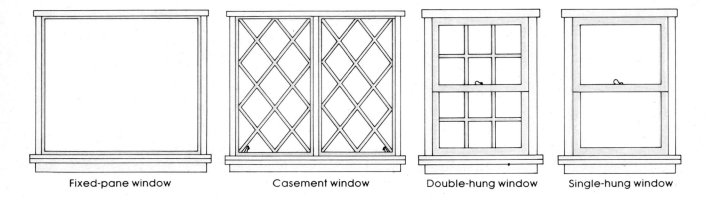

Fixed-pane window          Casement window          Double-hung window          Single-hung window

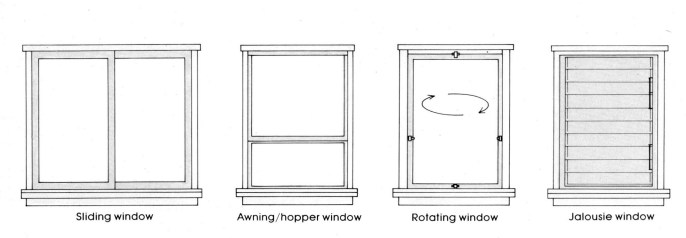

Sliding window          Awning/hopper window          Rotating window          Jalousie window

## Frames

| Frame material | Comments |
| --- | --- |
| **Aluminum** | Thermal-break variety eliminates transmission of heat or cold, which can cause condensation problems. Painting not needed, but color selection limited. |
| **Steel** | Uninsulated steel transmits cold and heat, which may result in condensation problems. Great durability if painted regularly to prevent rust. |
| **Wood** | Excellent insulating qualities. More expensive than other frames because individual craftsmanship required. Tighter seal than metal frames. Must be painted regularly. |
| **Vinyl-clad** | Wood windows—with all their qualities—covered with protective vinyl so no periodic painting is required. Vinyl is brittle in extreme cold. Wide variety of colors available. |

## Anatomy of a Window

The window illustrated here is double-hung; its moving parts make it one of the most complex types of windows. Older models contain sash balances, ropes, and pulleys, which can cause a window to jam when they don't work properly. Double-hung windows with such a system are no longer made except by special order. New models are made with a spring balance to hold the open window in place.

The double-hung window contains most of the components of other windows plus many of its own, making it a helpful index to window terms.

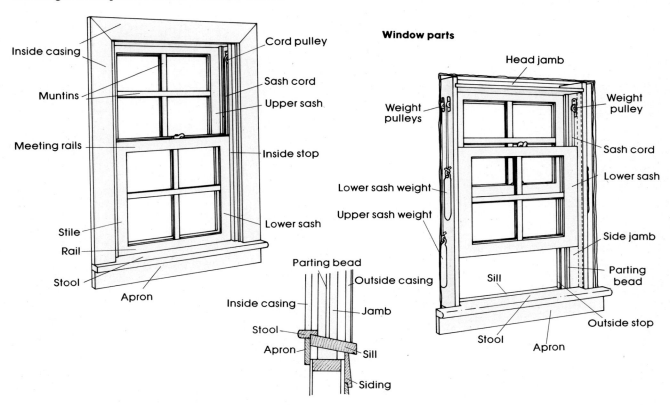

**Window parts**

## Glazing

You can have a window virtually any size, shape, or color you want. The most common choices are explained in the chart below; for special purposes, there are also safety and opaque glass and, of course, the decorative touch of stained glass. Whatever type of glazing you choose, there are different qualities and strengths of glass to be aware of.

| Glazing material | Comments |
| --- | --- |
| **Single-pane** | Least expensive glazing. Has poor thermal qualities. Commonly used in small-pane windows. |
| **Double-pane** | Factory-sealed dead air space between panes provides markedly improved thermal barrier. |
| **Tempered** | Provides needed additional strength for large picture windows, but still single-pane glass with poor thermal qualities. |
| **Plate** | High-quality, very hard glass used in sliding glass doors and shower doors to minimize chance of breakage. Expensive and with poor thermal qualities unless double-pane. |
| **Acrylic** | Virtually unbreakable. Clear initially, but scratches easily and dulls with age. |

It is said that into everyone's life a little rain must fall, but they don't tell you it usually comes when you decide to remove a window. Thus, have your new window on hand before taking out the old. However, to order the new window, you will need exact measurements of the rough opening. So start the process of removing the window by taking off the inside casing. With the rough opening revealed, measure the width, which is the distance between the inner edges of the trimmer studs, and the height, the distance between the rough sill and the bottom of the header. Since the opening may not be square, take several measurements. The window will be made to fit the narrowest ones. Obtain the new window before you proceed with removing the old one.

## Removing a Wood-Framed Window

The following instructions, for removing a double-hung window, apply to any wood-framed window. Work carefully to protect the wood, particularly the interior and exterior trim that you may reuse.

A double-hung window can be taken out from either the inside or the outside, whichever is more convenient. Start by removing the interior window trim. Carefully tap a broad chisel under one edge and gently pry it out. Don't pry the bottom all the way out, but work your way slowly upwards to avoid breaking the trim. If any nails are pulled through the trim and left in the trimmer studs, use a hammer to remove them.

Push both windows down. If the windows are hung by sash cords, cut them. If there is a spring-loaded balance, twist the metal top to loosen it. Now, with the chisel, pry off

**Measuring the rough opening**

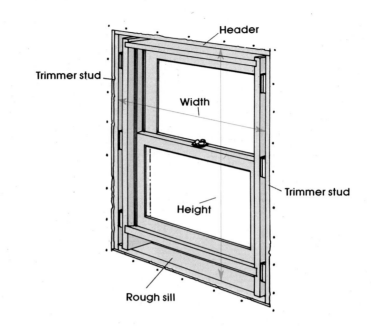

Header

Trimmer stud

Width

Height

Trimmer stud

Rough sill

**Removing a double-hung window**

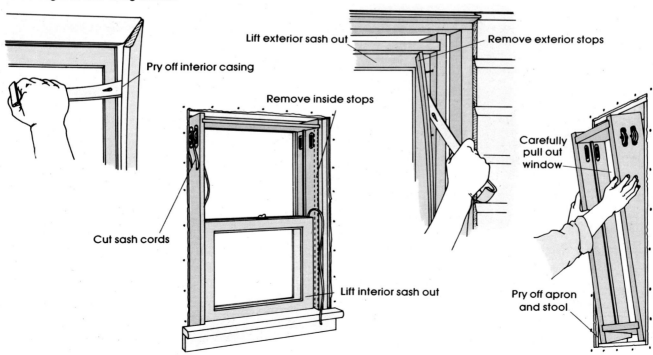

Pry off interior casing

Lift exterior sash out

Remove exterior stops

Remove inside stops

Cut sash cords

Carefully pull out window

Lift interior sash out

Pry off apron and stool

the interior stops and lift the interior sash out of the frame.

Working from inside, or outside if convenient, pry off the exterior trim. Again, work carefully here since it can be reused. Now remove the exterior stops. On spring-loaded sash balances, twist the metal top, pull off, and remove the spring. Take out the exterior sash.

Pry off the apron and the stool. If possible, pry off the jambs. It is sometimes easier to use a nail punch to drive the nails through the jambs and sill and lift the entire window unit out. Wrap the rough opening with flashing paper (see page 58 or 60, depending on the framing material of your new window).

## Removing a Nailing-Flange Window

Virtually all windows held in a metal frame, including fixed, casement, awning, jalousie, and rotating, have nailing flanges. Nailing flanges—called nail-on fins in the trade—extend out around the exterior part of the frame. The frame is set into the rough opening, the flanges nailed to the trimmer studs and header, and the siding covers the flanges. Trim then goes over the siding beside the window to cover the gap.

Here's how to remove these windows. Carefully pry off all the exterior trim so it can be reused. The flange is usually 1½ inches wide, so measure out 1¾ inches from the window frame all around and mark the outline on the siding. Set the blade on a circular saw to ⅛ inch deeper than the siding thickness. Use a carbide-tipped blade since you may hit some nails. Cut along the lines and then remove and save the siding pieces. Remove the nails from the flange and lift out the window.

Replace the flashing paper that should be around the rough window opening (follow the directions on pages 58 or 60, depending on the framing material of your new window). Put the siding pieces back against the window to fill the gap, caulk all cracks, and replace the trim.

**Removing a metal-framed window**

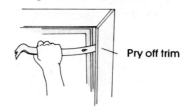

Pry off trim

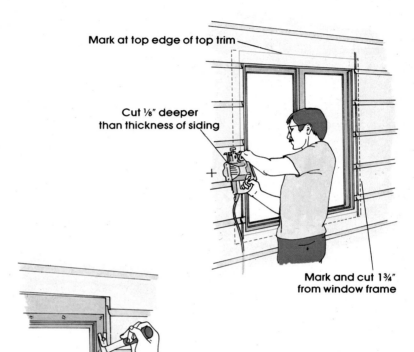

Mark at top edge of top trim

Cut ⅛" deeper than thickness of siding

Mark and cut 1¾" from window frame

Pull out all nails

Carefully lift window out

# FIXED-PANE WINDOW

When remodeling or building a new house, you may decide to open up a wall by installing a large fixed-pane window for both the view and the solar heat benefits. You may also be interested in the airtight qualities of fixed-pane windows, which, because they don't open, minimize air infiltration. For ventilation, one or more openable windows that are narrower but of the same height can be installed flanking the fixed windows.

There are many types of fixed-pane windows. They include large living-room picture windows, windows set next to French or sliding glass doors, stained glass windows, and most windows of unusual shape, such as diamonds and hexagons.

Fixed-pane windows can be purchased from custom window shops in any size or shape all made up and ready to install. They can be bought set into wood jambs that fit into the rough opening or in metal frames with nailing flanges. Buying windows already in frames makes them more convenient to install but adds to the cost. As an alternative, this section will take you through all the fundamentals of how to install your own fixed-pane window, including how to make and set a sill, how to build the jambs, and how to set the window. The job is somewhat complex, but still within the reach of the novice. Since careful workmanship is needed, consider a few practice runs by installing fixed windows in the garage, workshop, utility room, or a playhouse before attempting one in your living room.

## Choosing the Glass

The larger the window, the more area there is through which heat may escape. If you live in a moderate climate, you can use single-pane glass, which is quite economical and easy to handle. But in cold climates it will prove cost-effective to install glass with better thermal-conservation qualities.

Although it is technically possible to make your own double-pane glass, it is extremely difficult. You are much better off to order factory-sealed dual windows the size you need.

These windows are sold with either one or two sealants separating the glass. Better-quality windows have a double seal. In addition, both types have a dessicant—not to be confused with the sealant—inside the seal that absorbs any trapped moisture.

Dual windows used to be sold with an aluminum strip around the edges to hold them together, but that is not commonly found anymore. Instead, if you buy unframed thermal windows, they will be held together by the glue-like sealant. Handle the window with great care, so you don't break that seal or damage the window in any way.

## Framing the Opening

There are several ways to frame the rough openings for fixed windows. The most common way is to frame a standard opening, as described on page 9. Here you have the king studs, trimmer studs, header, and rough sill.

One alternative for a bank of high fixed windows along one wall

**Post-and-beam window framing**

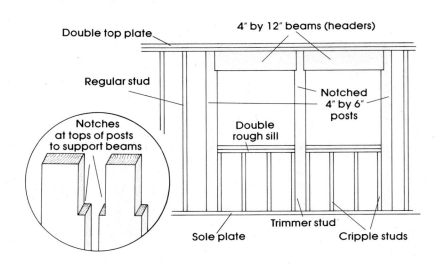

Double top plate · 4" by 12" beams (headers) · Regular stud · Notched 4" by 6" posts · Notches at tops of posts to support beams · Double rough sill · Sole plate · Trimmer stud · Cripple studs

**Windows between studs**

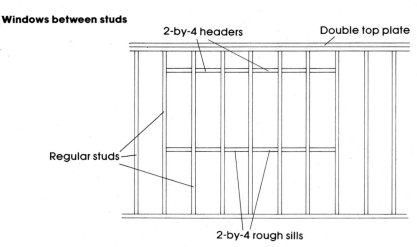

2-by-4 headers · Double top plate · Regular studs · 2-by-4 rough sills

**Two methods of installing the sill**

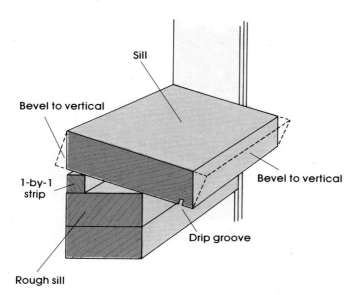

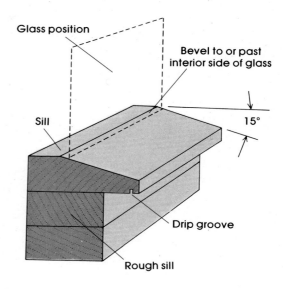

is a series of 4 by 6 support posts spaced 4 feet on center. The top ends are notched on each side as shown to accept lengths of 4 by 12s as headers; in rooms of standard height, 4 by 12s are commonly used as headers in door or window openings because they fit right under the top plate and no cripple studs are needed above them. The rough sill is set conventionally on cripple studs, since it will be covered by the interior wall material.

An even more unconventional way is to set the windows directly between studs. Here, no header is needed as long as you maintain standard stud spacing, which is 16 inches on center for 2 by 4s, and 24 inches on center for 2 by 6s. It may sound like this would chop up the view, but in fact the series of narrow windows breaks the view into attractive individually framed pictures.

If you choose to experiment with alternate methods, your primary consideration is to maintain proper structural support of the wall. That essentially involves headers of the correct size for the opening (see chart on page 8). If you are in any doubt, consult a licensed contractor or the building inspector.

**Installing the Window Sill**

The sill must be angled to shed water. Setting a fixed window on a level sill will surely cause water that is blown against the window to eventually leak inside. This not only stains the interior wall or stool, but can cause wood rot.

Sill material can be purchased at a hardware or lumber store or you can make your own quite easily. To make your own, choose 2-by stock that is at least 2 inches wider than the distance from interior to exterior wall. Before installing, set the blade on the circular saw to make a cut ¼ inch deep. Make this cut along the bottom of the exterior side of the sill about ½ inch from edge. This will prevent water from

running along the underside of the sill to the house.

The sill can be prepared in two different ways. In the first, as illustrated, the sill is raised on the interior side by resting on a length of 1 by 1. In this case, the edges must be beveled with a circular saw so that they are vertical when the sill is in place. Do this by setting the sill on the 1 by 1, then using a level to mark a vertical line along one end. Set the blade on your circular saw to that angle and cut. Flip the sill over and cut along the other edge.

Another way, which eliminates setting the sill on a 1 by 1, is to clamp it in a vise and then rip a bevel cut along the top exterior side. The angle need be only about 15 degrees, but it should extend to the interior side of the glass. A bevel only deep enough to reach the exterior side of the glass may allow water to creep underneath the pane. Once in place, the sill is covered on the interior by both the stool and the apron.

# FIXED-PANE WINDOW

**To Jamb or Not to Jamb**

Fixed-pane windows can be installed either with or without jambs. The better way is to construct jambs that frame the glass and are then set in the rough opening. The jambs can be shimmed to be square if the opening is not. In addition, the jambs are independent of the house structure and thus, if it shifts, the windows will remain in place. If the glass is set between framing members only and the house settles an inch or so, a gap may open up along one or more edges of the window.

On the other hand, it is much easier simply to place the windows between framing members rather than to construct and put together a number of jambs. Not all houses settle significantly, and the window can be recaulked if necessary.

**Installation Without a Jamb.** Windows are commonly installed without a jamb by one of the following two methods: using stops or using rabbets.

In an installation using stops, windows are set between verticals spaced 4 feet on center, and the glass is held in place between the verticals by ¾-inch stops on each side of the glass. A standard header and rough sill must be installed.

First put the sill in place on the rough sill. Position the inside stops by measuring in 1½ inches from the outside edge (the thickness of two ¾-inch stops), plus the thickness of the glass (usually ⅝ inch for double-panes), *plus* ¼ inch. The additional ¼ inch allows a ⅛-inch clearance on both sides of the glass for a strip of butyl glazing tape all around the window. The butyl rubber tape, available at glazing outlets, not only acts as a seal but remains pliant and allows the wood to expand or contract without disturbing the window pane.

**No-jamb installation using stops**

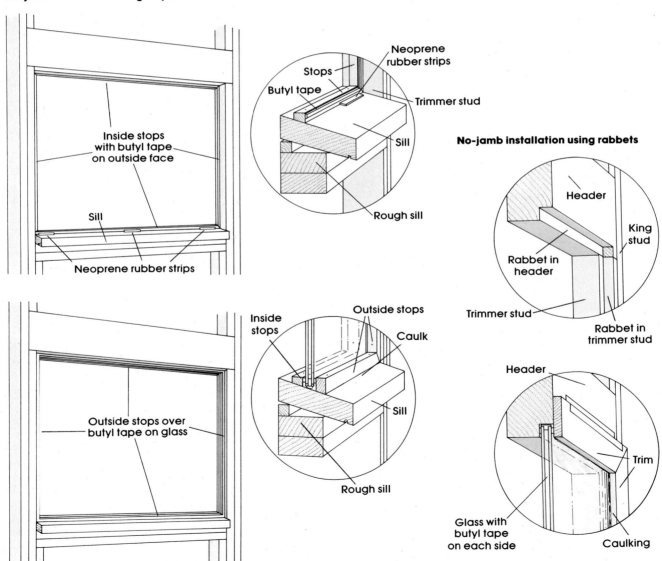

No-jamb installation using rabbets

Once the measurements are made and marked, nail 1 by 1 stock (actually ¾ inches by ¾ inches) around the window opening to form the inside stops. Note that the bottom stop is beveled at an angle to match the sill. Lay a narrow strip of butyl tape around the stop where the glass will fit against it.

Cut three strips of neoprene rubber (available at glaziers) the same thickness as the glass, 4 inches long. Place these strips, which cushion the glass, on the sill next to the bottom stop, one at each side and one in the center.

With a helper, put the glass in place against the stops and resting on the neoprene strips. While your helper holds it, go around the outside window edges with a strip of butyl tape.

Put the outside stops in place snug against the butyl tape but not crushing it, and nail. In this particular style, no exterior trim is used around the window.

The second method, using rabbets, is a modification of the first. A more finished appearance is obtained by using dado blades on a table saw, or a router, to cut a rabbet around the edges of the support posts and the header. Make the rabbet ½ inch wide and as deep as the glass is thick, plus ¼ inch for the butyl tape. Apply the tape to the rabbet where the pane will fit, and put the neoprene strips in place on the sill.

With the help of a second person, put the glass in place and put the butyl tape around the outside edge of the glass.

Nail the exterior trim (such as 1-by-3 redwood or cedar if unpainted) in place so that it overlaps the window by ½ inch, the same amount as the rabbet. Apply caulk (see page 76) to seal the gap between the trim and the glass.

**Installation with a Jamb.** A jamb allows you to set a window in an opening that is not square. Make the jamb from kiln-dried wood, if available, so that it will not warp as it dries. Use 2-by stock wide enough

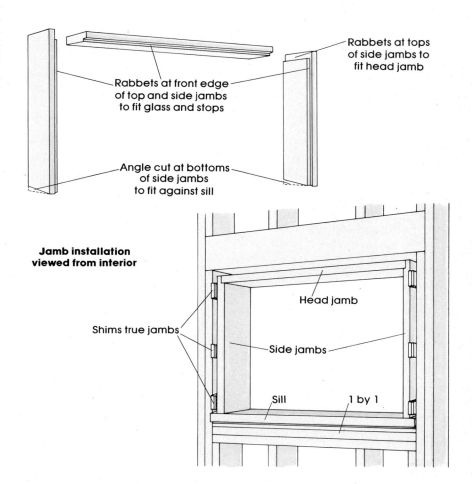

**Jamb installation viewed from exterior**

Rabbets at tops of side jambs to fit head jamb

Rabbets at front edge of top and side jambs to fit glass and stops

Angle cut at bottoms of side jambs to fit against sill

**Jamb installation viewed from interior**

Shims true jambs

Head jamb

Side jambs

Sill

1 by 1

to cover the opening from the interior to the exterior siding. You probably will have to use lumber that is wider and rip it to your particular measurements.

With a table saw and dado blade, or a router, rabbet the exterior edges of the jamb stock. The rabbet should be cut to a depth equal to half the size of the outside stops. The width of the rabbet should be ¾ inch for the outside stop, plus the thickness of the glass, plus ¼ inch for the butyl tape on both sides.

Construct the jamb for the size of your glass as shown, with the side jambs rabbeted on the tops so the head jamb is flush with the tops. Construct the jamb so there will be ½-inch clearance from the rough opening on the two sides and the top. No jamb material is needed on

the bottom, but the sill must be perfectly level. If it isn't, shim it on one side to level it.

Place the jamb in the rough opening and place shingle shims from inside and outside to secure the jamb. Use a steel square in the corners to check that it is square, and a level to ensure that it is plumb. Nail it in place through the shingle shims.

Put neoprene strips on the sill, put the butyl tape in the rabbet where the glass will press against it, then put the glass in place.

While the helper holds the glass, tape the exterior edges of the glass and then nail on the stops. Caulk along the edges between the stops and the glass, then install the trim around the window (see pages 40–41) Finally, put on the stool, apron, and interior trim.

# WOOD-FRAMED WINDOW

### Choosing the Window

Double- and single-hung windows are made up in either wood or metal frames. This section deals with installation of the more complicated wood-framed windows. Most wood-framed windows, of whatever style, are installed in this fashion. Metal-framed windows, which have nail-on fins, are installed in a different manner, covered on page 60.

Double-hung windows consist of two sashes that slide up and down in a frame; in a single-hung window, one sash is fixed. Older types of these windows are held in place by a system of counter-weights, ropes, and pulleys that are set in pockets on each side of the window opening. Newer double- and single-hung windows are held in the open position by spring-powered balances.

However, the counter-weight system remains in thousands of homes. If your home has one, you need to know how to maintain and repair it (pages 89–90). Replacing it with a modern window is covered in this section. These instructions also

apply to installing a wood-framed window in new construction. Instructions for installing metal-framed windows are on page 60.

If your window is a standard size, you can find one ready-made that will fit. But custom-fit windows can be made up in window shops at a comparable price, so shop around. If you are replacing only a few windows, they should be made up to match existing ones.

Whether your new window is ready-made or custom-fit, its size will be based on the rough opening (see page 52 for measuring the rough opening). Different manufacturers specify different gaps between the window jamb and rough opening to allow for shimming; it is usually ¼ inch to ½ inch.

If you want the sashes and lights in the new windows to match those of other similar windows in the house, be sure to measure the others and give the dimensions to the window shop.

Although a window can be made to fit your opening, the wood frame material may not match the

depth of your overall wall thickness, which is from exterior to interior covering. (This problem does not exist with metal-framed windows.) The interior of the window jamb must be flush with the inside wall covering. If the frame is not deep enough, you must use jamb extenders; if it is too long, you will use filler strips. Both are explained below.

### Installing the Window

If the old window opening had pockets along the sides for counterweights, fill the holes loosely with insulation. Don't pack it in, since the air trapped in the insulation provides the protection.

Before the new window is installed, it should be squared. Lay it face down on a flat surface, then place a steel framing square inside the corners. Both sides of the square should rest flush against the window jambs. If they don't, push at diagonal corners of the window until it is square. Then tack two thin pieces of wood across two corners to hold it square. Trim off any overhang so the frame can be inserted into the rough opening.

Wrap the studs forming the rough opening with flashing paper. Slip one edge under the siding, then bend the paper around the trimmer studs, rough sill, and header, and staple in place.

Next, a piece of aluminum flashing should be cut to match the window width. Scribe a line ¾ inch in from one edge, bend the edge up at a 90-degree angle, and slip it up under the siding at the top of the opening. The flashing that protrudes should be long enough to overlap the top edge of the window frame by ½ inch. When the window is in place, bend this down over the top trim.

Now put the window in place. While a helper holds it there, check that the frame is flush with the interior wall. If it extends into the room, push it back flush with the wall. Now, outside, measure the gap between the siding and the exterior trim on the window frame. Cut filler strips that width and insert. The strips should be no wider than the exterior trim.

**Squaring the window**

**Wood-framed window installation**

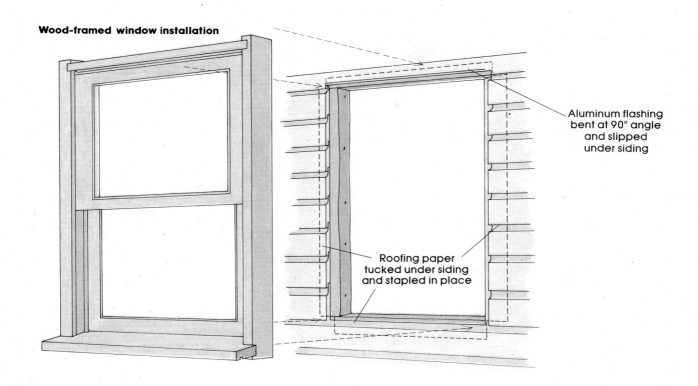

Aluminum flashing bent at 90° angle and slipped under siding

Roofing paper tucked under siding and stapled in place

**Using a filler strip**

**Using a jamb extender**

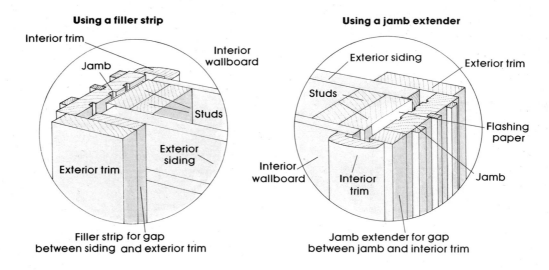

Interior trim

Jamb

Interior wallboard

Studs

Exterior trim

Exterior siding

Filler strip for gap between siding and exterior trim

Exterior siding

Exterior trim

Studs

Flashing paper

Interior wallboard

Interior trim

Jamb

Jamb extender for gap between jamb and interior trim

If the window frame is short of the interior wall, measure the differences and cut jamb extenders the same width as the frame material to fill this gap. In some cases, jamb extenders come with the window. If they protrude slightly beyond the wall, plane them down with a jack plane and nail in place.

With everything ready, have a helper press the window in place again while you center it in the opening from inside. Use shingle shims to raise the window sill from the rough sill until the gap equals that between the header jamb and rough header. Place a level on the sill to check it, and shim both sides to wedge the window in place. With 8d casing nails, nail the sill to the rough sill through the shims. Nail the jambs to the trimmer studs with 12d casing nails placed through the exterior stops. Sink the nails below the wood surface with a nail set, then fill the holes with color-matching wood putty.

Bend the flashing over the top of the exterior casing, then run a bead of caulk between the exterior trim and siding.

For installation of interior trim, stool, and apron, see pages 40–41.

# METAL-FRAMED WINDOW

## Choosing the Window

The metal window frame with a nail-on fin, or flange, is used for virtually every type of window there is, from fixed-pane to double-hung to casement to sliding. Among its advantages over wood-framed windows are lower price, fast and easy installation, and a sturdy rot-proof construction. Among its drawbacks are aesthetics—you have a metal frame instead of the warmer-appearing wood. Unless you choose thermal-break frames, you will also suffer energy loss; metal frames transmit cold into the house much more than wood does. Choices of color in aluminum frames are also quite limited, usually only natural or bronzed; steel frames must be kept painted to prevent rust.

All styles are made up with either single or dual glass according to your specifications. Before ordering any for new construction, check your local codes, since many areas now require dual windows to cut energy bills.

## Installing the Window

**New Construction.** Window frames are shipped with the sashes in place. Keep them closed and locked while installing.

Manufacturers make up your window fractionally smaller than the size you specify, which will give you all the clearance you need. Thus, for a window 3 feet wide you will have a rough opening just 3 feet wide, with no additional clearance. The instructions that follow are for new construction or replacing one metal-framed window with another. For replacing a wood-framed window with a metal-framed one, see below.

The first installation step is to cover the edges of the rough opening with flashing paper. Note in the illustration how it is stapled in place, putting the bottom strip on first, with the two side strips overlapping the bottom strip and extending 6 inches above the window height. The top strip goes on after the window is installed and overlaps the nail-on fin.

Once the flashing is up, the actual installation is quite simple. Run a bead of caulking around the inside of the fin. Then have a helper put the window in place, with the nail-on fins tight against the rough opening. From inside, use shingle shims to raise the window until the gaps at top and bottom are equal. Center the window so there are equal gaps on both sides.

Place a level on the bottom edge of the frame; adjust the frame until it is perfectly level. Now open the sash to see that it operates smoothly and closes evenly.

Hold the window firmly in place, then drive 8d nails through the flanges into the rough opening frame. Space nails every 12 inches.

Staple the flashing paper across the top.

When the siding is installed, it should be fitted over the flange and snug against the window frame. Run a bead of caulk between the siding and frame; then put trim around the window over the siding.

**Replacing a Wood-framed Window.** When installing a nail-on fin window in place of a wood-framed window, the first job after the old window is removed is to cut away the siding around the rough opening by ¼ inch more than the width of the flange, or about 1¾ inches. Measure and mark the outline on one siding, using a level so the lines are plumb and level. Set the blade on the circular saw ⅛ inch deeper than the siding thickness and then cut. Save these pieces.

Install the window as described above, then nail the siding pieces back in place over the flange. Caulk the gap between the window and the siding pieces and caulk the line where you made the cut.

The final step is to nail the trim back around the window.

**Metal-framed window installation**

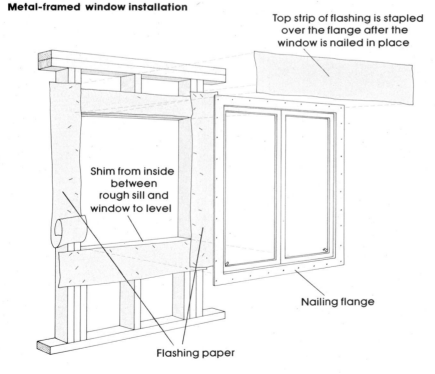

Top strip of flashing is stapled over the flange after the window is nailed in place

Shim from inside between rough sill and window to level

Nailing flange

Flashing paper

# INSTALLING A
# GREENHOUSE WINDOW

**Greenhouse window installation**

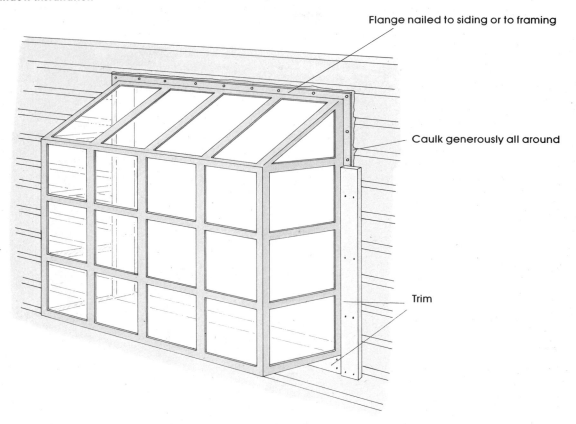

Flange nailed to siding or to framing

Caulk generously all around

Trim

## Choosing the Best Location

Ideally, the window should catch the low winter sun in the south, but be protected from long periods of direct summer sun. Since the window does not extend out far, the overhanging eaves on your house may provide the necessary shade during the summer months. If not, roll-up bamboo or vinyl blinds can be hung in front of it. Also available at most nurseries is shade cloth that filters the sunlight from 30 percent to 80 percent, depending on the density of the weave. Proper shading of greenhouse windows is important, since overheating is one of their biggest problems.

Greenhouse windows can also be placed on the east side of the house, where many kitchens are located, to catch the morning sun but be protected from long afternoon sun.

For more information on greenhouses and how they work, see Ortho's book, *How to Build & Use Greenhouses.*

## Choosing the Window

A greenhouse window is an attractive and practical addition to any window, but it is particularly nice in the kitchen. A variety of herbs and flowers can be kept growing in it year-round to provide culinary treats and color. Even though the greenhouse window extends out only 16 inches at most, its open design visually enlarges the room.

Aluminum-framed greenhouse windows are commonly sold through glass and window outlets. They come in standard sizes or can be made to fit your particular need. They are constructed with either single-pane or insulating glass, with the latter obviously minimizing heat loss through the glass. But thermal panes cost more, so be the judge of your needs according to your climate.

Another factor that should be considered when thinking about a greenhouse window is its venting system. This aspect is essential during hot weather to protect the

plants. The most efficient vents are those with side casement or sliding windows that provide cross ventilation. A single vent at the top to release hot air is just as good. Less useful is a ventilation system with small windows opening only at the bottom of the sides. The hot air at the top of the window cannot escape to the outside but instead is pushed back into the house.

To order a greenhouse window, whether ready-made or custom-fit, you must have the rough opening measurements (see page 52). Virtually all greenhouse windows are metal, with nail-on fins.

## Installing the Window

The standard greenhouse window has a metal frame with nail-on fins around the edges. It is installed in the same manner as all such windows, as described on the opposite page.

Although the greenhouse window protrudes from the side of the house, it is lightweight and no additional supports are needed.

# SKYLIGHT

## Choosing the Best Location

In planning a skylight location, you may not have a lot of choice. But if you do, consider the kind of light you'll be letting in. On a roof slope facing south or west, the skylight will admit a lot of direct summer sun. That can increase room temperature and fade rugs and furniture. Placing it on an east or north slope will give you just as much light but less direct sun. If you must place a skylight where it will receive a lot of direct sunlight, you can choose one that is tinted.

## Choosing the Skylight

Skylights usually range in widths from 16 inches to 4 feet, and in lengths from 2 feet to 6 feet, but you can have them custom made at window shops to fit nearly any opening. Smaller ones, which are less expensive, generally admit ample light. In addition, skylights that are only 2 feet wide will fit between most rafters, which simplifies installation. You can also increase the amount of light if your installation requires a light well (also called a light shaft) between the roof and the ceiling. The lightwell can be angled or splayed (see illustrations).

Another consideration is what type of skylight you want. Some have a tinted bubble to reduce light; others have a frosted bubble to diffuse the sunlight, while others have clear plastic or glass.

There are single-wall and double-wall bubbles, the latter having a dead-air space for insulation—a good choice in cold climates.

Some skylights open to provide summer ventilation. The more elaborate of these are operated electrically through thermostats set at a temperature of your choice.

Some skylights are self-flashing, which means they are quite simple to install, but some roofing professionals consider them slightly more prone to leaks. The other style is mounted over a wood framework, called a curb, which must be flashed.

Whatever you decide on, do some comparative shopping because prices vary considerably.

**Lightwell shapes**

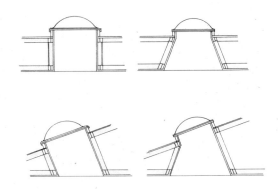

**Skylight curb**

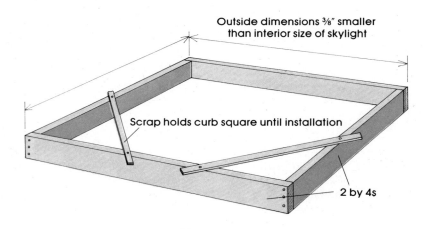

Outside dimensions ⅜" smaller than interior size of skylight

Scrap holds curb square until installation

2 by 4s

The more complex skylight is the curb-mounted style, for which instructions follow. Details on the self-flashing skylight are covered on page 66.

## Framing the Opening for the Curb-Mounted Skylight

First, a word of caution: weather. A skylight can usually be installed in a single day. But you should be prepared for rain. Have on hand a tarp or plastic sheet large enough to reach from 2 feet below the opening to 4 feet over the ridge, and lumber or bricks to weight the edges.

**Constructing the Curb.** In order to create the opening, you must first build the curb. It is made from 2 by 4s as illustrated. Measure and cut carefully so that it is ⅜ inch smaller all around than the interior dimension of the skylight. This allows the skylight to fit over both the curb and its step flashing.

When the curb is nailed together, square it with a framing square; then tack two light pieces of wood across the diagonal corners to hold it in position.

A skylight normally is positioned in the roof so that it and its light shaft will be centered in the ceiling of the room below. If no ceiling is involved, and thus no light shaft, half your construction problems are eliminated. Where a ceiling is involved, decide where you want the center point of the light shaft to be and drive a nail through

## Skylight framing patterns

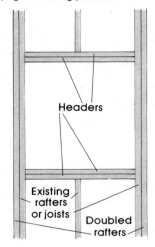
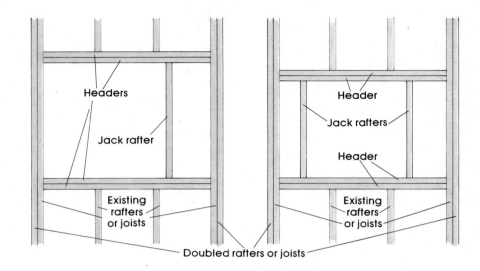

Headers

Headers

Header

Jack rafter

Jack rafters

Header

Existing
rafters
or joists

Doubled
rafters

Existing
rafters
or joists

Existing
rafters
or joists

Doubled rafters or joists

the ceiling there. In the attic, drop a plumb bob from the underside of the roof deck to the nail in the ceiling to find the center of the roof opening. If need be, move this point a few inches to eliminate unnecessary cutting of rafters or joists. Try to line up one side of the skylight on an existing rafter.

From the illustrations you can see the different patterns of framing an opening, depending on your particular needs. The simplest way is to use existing rafters rather than building in one or more jack rafters.

Once you have found the center point on the roof deck, mark the *inside* curb dimensions across the rafters and the underside of the roof deck. Do this with a framing square and careful measurements. At each corner mark, drive a nail to protrude above the roof.

Now measure down 3 inches below the bottom line of the curb outline (toward the eaves) and 3 inches above it (toward the ridge). Snap straight lines across the rafter bottom(s) at these marks. The additional 3 inches above and below allows for the double headers that will be installed between the rafters. The intervening rafters will be cut on these lines.

Before you cut, support the rafters by nailing 2 by 4s to them above and below the marks, with the bottoms of the supports resting on ceiling joists and toenailed in place. The opening in the roof can

### Finding the center of the roof opening

Use a plumb bob and string to mark center of skylight on roof decking

Nail marks center of ceiling opening

### Supporting the rafters

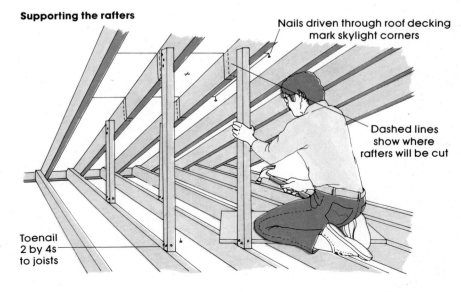

Nails driven through roof decking mark skylight corners

Dashed lines show where rafters will be cut

Toenail 2 by 4s to joists

# SKYLIGHT

be cut now, or you can wait until you've finished the interior framing. When you do cut it, you might want a friend stationed below to help you with the cut-out piece.

When you're ready to cut the opening in the roof, snap chalklines to connect all the nail points. The inside corners of the curb will be where the nails came through the roof. The outside edge of the curb will be 1½ inches outside the nails. To give yourself a little room to work, snap another chalkline 2 inches outside the first one. Cut the shingles on this line.

Set the blade of your circular saw the depth of the roofing shingles and then cut along the lines.

Remove the shingles. Snap new lines on the roof deck, using the nail holes as guides. Set the blade on your saw to ⅛ inch more than the thickness of the roof deck and cut along the lines. Remove the decking.

Back inside the attic, cut any rafter that crosses the opening on the chalklines you made 3 inches above and below the curb outline. Measure the distance at the top and bottom between the two uncut rafters nearest the sides of the opening. Cut four header boards this length from the same-size stock as the rafters. At the top or bottom of the opening, fit a header board between the two existing uncut rafters. Nail through the rafters into the ends of the header with 16d nails. Nail the middle section of the header to the end(s) of the cut rafter(s). Do the same at the other end of the opening. Now nail each second header in place over the first one in the same manner. Install any jack rafters needed. The roof opening is now framed. Remove the braces.

If you planned a lightwell that is angled or splayed, cut the rafters at the corresponding angle before installing the headers.

## Installing the Curb-Mounted Skylight

Set the curb over the opening, double-check that it is centered and square, then toenail it from the inside through the roof and deck and into the rafters and headers.

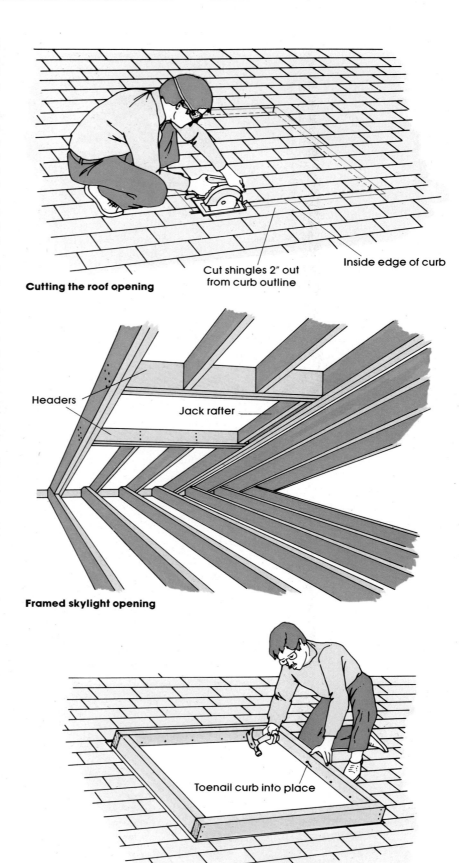

**Cutting the roof opening**

Cut shingles 2" out from curb outline

Inside edge of curb

Headers

Jack rafter

**Framed skylight opening**

Toenail curb into place

**Installing the curb**

## Flashing a Curb

Some skylights are sold with a flashing kit as an optional extra. If the kit includes strip flashing along the sides, reject it and buy or make your own step flashing. It is the only way to be sure the skylight won't leak.

Curb flashing is often called saddle flashing, a term that refers to the way the head and base flashing fit around the top and bottom of the curb. If you give the outside measurements of the curb to a sheet metal shop, they will make up the flashing for you.

To install the flashing, first fit the base flashing in a bed of cement around the bottom edge of the curb. Nail it along the top of the curb. Note that the apron rests on top of the shingle course along the bottom edge of the curb.

Fit the first piece of step flashing overlapping the base flashing. Slide it beneath the shingle, embedding the edge next to the curb in roofing cement. Nail it to the curb along the top edge. Continue up both sides in this fashion until you reach the top. Fit the head flashing around the top of the curb and embed it in cement, then nail. Spread roofing cement around the top and side edges of the apron that extends onto the roof deck, then nail the shingle courses down over it. Set each shingle edge in roofing cement for added protection.

**Flashing components**

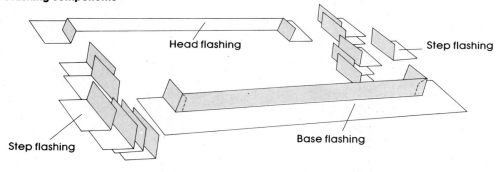

Head flashing

Step flashing

Step flashing

Base flashing

**Curb-flashing installation**

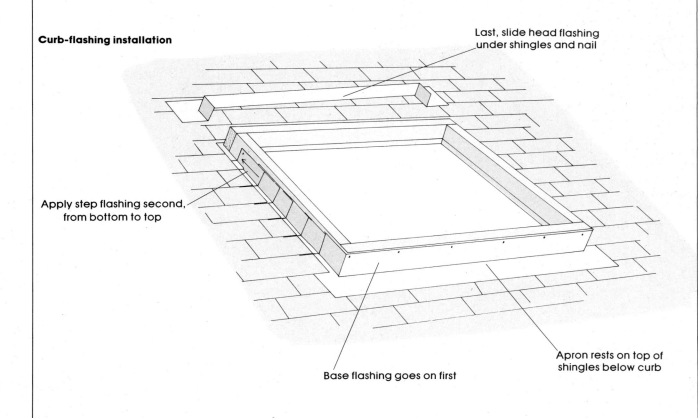

Last, slide head flashing under shingles and nail

Apply step flashing second, from bottom to top

Base flashing goes on first

Apron rests on top of shingles below curb

**Setting the curb-mounted skylight in place**

Caulking

**Self-flashing skylight installation**

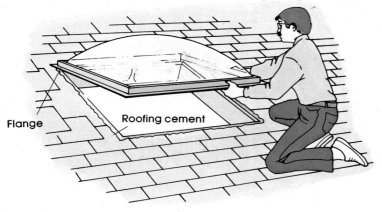

Flange

Roofing cement

**Supporting the ceiling joists**

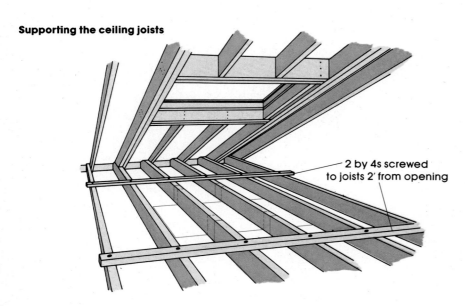

2 by 4s screwed
to joists 2' from opening

Install the flashing (see box, page 65). Apply a bead of caulking or some cushioned weatherstripping to the top of the curb, then drop the skylight over the curb and flashing, and nail it to the curb along the upper edge or through the factory-drilled holes. Cover each nail head with a dab of roofing cement.

### Installing the Self-Flashing Skylight

The opening for the self-flashing skylight is located in the same manner as above, and the opening is constructed in the same fashion. The opening should be the same as the inside dimensions; do not cut outside the chalkline as you would for the curb-mounted one.

Remove the shingles around the sides and top of the opening so the flashing flange lies flat on the roof deck. The lower part of the flange lies on *top* of the shingles. Coat the deck with roofing cement, then press the flange into it. Check that the skylight is centered and square, then nail down the top and sides (not the bottom) of the flange with roofing nails spaced 6 inches apart. Coat the edges and the top of the flashing flange with cement; then replace the shingles around the skylight. As a final touch, lay a bead of caulk or roofing cement along the edges of the shingles where they fit next to the skylight.

### Constructing a Lightwell

With the skylight in place, you can open the ceiling and finish the lightwell without fear of rain.

The first step is to frame the ceiling opening, which can be done before cutting the ceiling. First, support the ceiling joists. Do this by laying two 2 by 4s flat across the joists 2 feet back from the planned opening. They should reach two rafters beyond any that must be cut. Drill holes through the 2 by 4s and into the top of each joist, then fasten them with 4-inch screws.

To frame the ceiling opening, follow the same procedure that was used to frame the skylight opening.

Once the framing is complete, cut out the ceiling opening by punching a drywall saw through the wallboard from above and cutting along the edge of the framing material.

The light shaft is constructed with 2 by 4s, spaced not more than 24 inches apart on center. The tops of the 2 by 4s are toenailed to the rafters and the bottoms to the joists. If you have installed a wide skylight, with jack rafters and jack joists, they will line up directly above and below each other. But if you have a skylight designed to fit between two existing rafters, you run into a little problem. Note that since ceiling joists are nailed to the sides of rafters where they meet on the cap plate of the stud wall, they are not lined up directly under the rafters. To achieve an uninterrupted surface in the lightwell, study the illustration. The 2 by 4s on one side are nailed to the side of a joist and toenailed to the bottom of a rafter. On the other side the 2 by 4s are nailed to the face of the rafter and toenailed to the top of the joist. The framework now falls smoothly from the skylight opening.

One or more angles must be cut at the top and bottom of the 2 by 4s, depending on what angle you chose for the lightwell. Cut the 2 by 4s a couple of inches less than the measured distance from the roof deck to the ceiling at roughly the desired angle. Place the 2 by 4s against the rafters and joists at the precise angle, then mark the 2 by 4s where they cross the rafter and joist. Cut along that line; then toenail the 2 by 4s to either the rafter or joist, depending on which side of the opening they are on. At each corner, nail another 2 by 4 on the back edge of the corner supports to provide a nailing surface for the drywall.

Staple insulation batts around the lightwell with the foil facing the lightwell.

Finish the lightwell by covering its interior with paneling to match the room or with drywall taped and painted a light color for good light reflection.

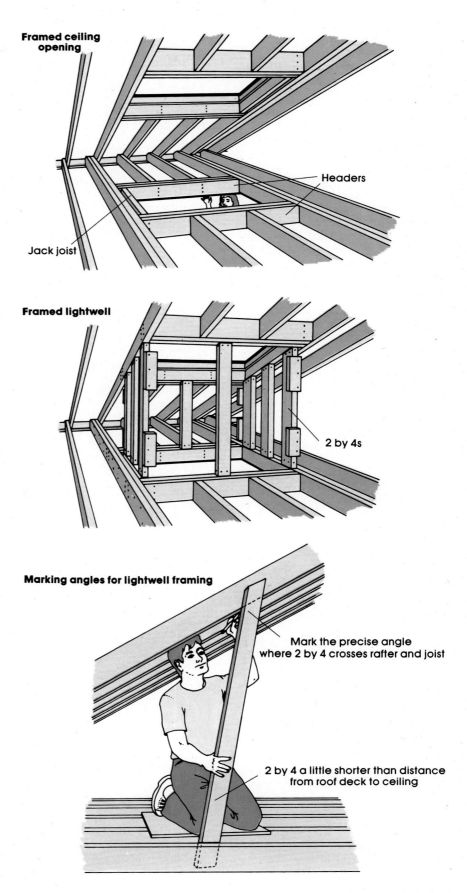

**Framed ceiling opening**

Headers

Jack joist

**Framed lightwell**

2 by 4s

**Marking angles for lightwell framing**

Mark the precise angle where 2 by 4 crosses rafter and joist

2 by 4 a little shorter than distance from roof deck to ceiling

# BAY WINDOW

## Choosing the Window

A bay window can be installed in two basic ways: by simply inserting it in a standard window opening, or by altering the wall beneath it to conform to the lines of the window. The latter involves more construction, but it opens up the room significantly, and a small seating area can be installed in the alcove.

Bay windows can be purchased already made up in standard sizes, made to your specifications, or in a kit form that you assemble. Unless the window fits tightly against a soffit under the overhanging eaves, a roof must also be installed. If you are buying a ready-made unit or a kit, check with your dealer to find out if a precut roof comes with the unit or if one must be built separately.

## Installing a Bay Window in a Window Opening

A bay window is installed into an opening in much the same way as a standard window is, whether it is wood-framed or metal-framed. It is, of course, heavier and larger, so have two or three friends on hand to assist. If the window opening must be made larger or smaller to fit the window size you chose, follow the instructions on page 15.

Note that bay window styles are made to fit either against the existing siding or against the wall sheathing. Be sure to follow the specifications that come with the window to prepare the house exterior to accommodate the window.

Once the window opening is ready, have the helpers set the window in the opening from the outside and hold it there. From the inside, place a level on the window stool and use shingle shims to level it. When the window is level, nail the stool to the rough window sill through the shims.

Use the level to check the plumb on both sides of the window. Use shims to make any adjustments and to attain a snug fit. On wood-framed windows, nail the sides through any shims to the trimmer studs on either side. On metal-framed windows, nail the flanges to the house exterior.

Finally, use shims between the headboard and the header for a snug fit and then nail.

The bay window may have to be supported underneath with knee braces. Instructions with the window unit will specify if they are needed. If they are, and the manufacturer did not supply them, make the knee braces as shown from 2 by 4s or decoratively cut 2 by 12s. Attach them to the house with lag bolts sunk into studs. Fasten the top of the brace to the bottom of the frame with wood screws. Metal-framed bay windows of this style generally do not need braces.

**Installing a Precut Roof.** To install a precut roof, first tack the wooden drip edge around the top of the bay window. Fit the front and sides of the roof together on top of the bay window, then mark the roof's outline where it fits against the house siding. Set the blade on your circular saw to the depth of the siding, and cut along the lines. Remove the siding. Fit the roof together against the side of the house and mark the outline on the roofing felt that wraps the house. (If there is none, cover the opening with 15-pound felt cut to fit. Staple it to the studs.) Measure the thickness of the plywood roofing and snap new lines that distance inside the outline of the roof. The end rafters, hip rafters, and common rafters will be installed so the top edges fall along these inner lines.

Before installing the rafters, provide some additional window support by tying the top of the window to the house with plumber's tape, available at hardware stores. Use wood screws with a washer to attach the metal straps from the edge of the frame to a stud.

The next step is to nail the rafters in place, starting with the two hip rafters. The two hip rafters must be beveled along the top outer edge, so that the side pieces of the roof will fit smoothly against the front piece. Use a jack plane to make the bevel if you discover that

**Knee braces**

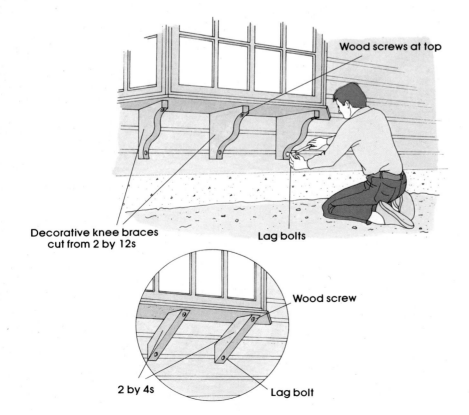

Decorative knee braces cut from 2 by 12s

Wood screws at top

Lag bolts

Wood screw

2 by 4s

Lag bolt

**Adding support for bay window**

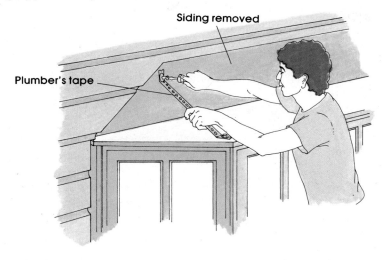

Siding removed

Plumber's tape

**Bay window roof installation**

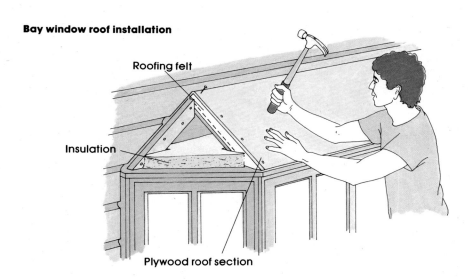

Roofing felt

Insulation

Plywood roof section

**Bay window roof flashing**

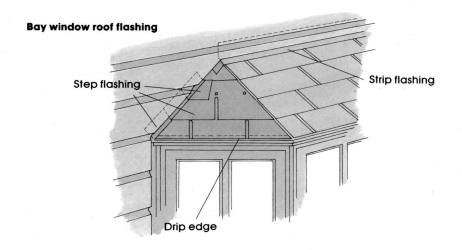

Step flashing

Strip flashing

Drip edge

it has not already been done.

When the rafters are installed, lay in a length of insulation over the top of the window, with the foil face down. Put the roof in place and nail it to the rafters. Nail metal drip edges around the base of the roof, then cover it with 15-pound roofing felt. Overlap the hips and staple.

Cover the roof to match your existing roof.

The roof must be flashed where it joins the side of the house. Step flashing is used where the roof slopes down on each side against the house, and a single length of strip flashing is used across the top. The same method is used for all roof types—tile, composition shingles, shakes, or wood shingles.

Step flashing is cut from 10-inch-long aluminum strips that are as wide as the exposure of your shingles (the distance from the base of one shingle to the base of the one above). On composition shingles, this exposure is normally 5 inches, as it is for wood shingles; for shakes, the exposure is usually 7 inches. Have the flashing made up at a local sheet metal shop.

From the illustration, you can see how the first piece of flashing is slipped up under the siding and then covered by the doubled first row of shingles. The second piece of flashing is slipped under the siding and spaced the distance of the shingle exposure, then covered by the second row of shingles. Continue up both sides in this manner. Next apply the hip shingles. For more details on applying roofing, see Ortho's book, *How to Replace & Install Roofs and Sidings.*

The final step is applying the strip flashing across the top. Cut a length of flashing 6 inches to 8 inches wide and as long as the roof plus 3-inch ears on each end as shown. Bend it lengthwise in the middle, and slip one part under the siding. Coat the top of the last row of shingles with roofing cement, then press the flashing into the cement. Coat the underside of the ears with cement and bend over the hip shingles. Finally, run a thick bead of caulk along the gap between the siding and shingles.

## Creating a Bay Window Alcove

Altering an exterior wall to create an alcove that conforms to the bay window is more complex than simply installing a bay window in an opening. But the effort will prove worthwhile. The alcove gives a new dimension to the room. It can provide a snug hideaway for reading on relaxed afternoons or it can become a seating area for a cozy breakfast nook.

The alcove is supported by cantilevered joists the same size as existing ones that extend over the foundation wall to give it a floating effect. Before you begin any construction, go under your house and determine which way the floor joists run. Depending on the direction, use the appropriate tie-in method described below.

**Supporting on Parallel Joists.** If the joists of the house run parallel to the joists that will support the alcove, your construction work is made easier. The support joists will be simply nailed to the existing ones.

Measure the height and width of the bay window opening and mark it out on the interior wall to be removed. Remove the interior wall and frame the rough opening as you would a door opening, described on page 8.

From inside, drive nails through the exterior siding at each corner, then snap chalk lines from nail to nail to mark the opening on the outside wall.

Remove the siding along the bottom of the opening to expose the floor joists. The joists are secured in one of two ways: with a rim joist that extends the length of the building and covers the ends of the joists, or with blocks placed between the ends of the joists. In the first case, cut through the rim joist flush with the edge of the last joist on each side of the opening and pry out that section of rim joist. It is nailed to the ends of the joists. In the second case, the blocks are toenailed to the sides of the joists. Cut in the middle of each block to be removed, pry out the pieces, then pull any nails remaining in the joists.

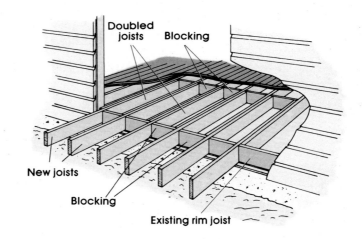

**Alcove support with parallel joists**

Doubled joists
Blocking
New joists
Blocking
Existing rim joist

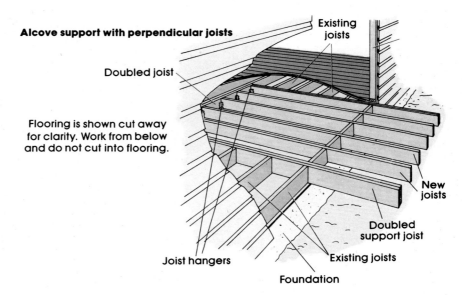

**Alcove support with perpendicular joists**

Existing joists
Doubled joist

Flooring is shown cut away for clarity. Work from below and do not cut into flooring.

New joists
Doubled support joist
Joist hangers
Existing joists
Foundation

Measure the total depth of the bay window, then cut joists three times that length. If, for instance, the bay window extends 24 inches, then cut the supporting joists 72 inches long. Hammer the support joists into position beside the existing ones, with one third of the length extending out from the house and the other two thirds nailed to the existing joists.

**Supporting on Perpendicular Joists.** When the floor joists run at right angles to the planned alcove joists, sections of several floor joists must be removed to make room for the alcove joists.

The support joists will reach under the floor at least twice the depth of the alcove overhang. Thus, if the bay window extends out 2 feet, you must remove sections of joists at least 4 feet back under the house. Determine how many joists must be cut. The next full joist will support the alcove joists and must be reinforced with a joist long enough to be supported on either end by the foundation wall or a girder. Wedge the reinforcing joist in place on the back side of the existing joist, then nail it to the existing joist.

The existing floor joists must be supported on both sides of the planned opening before any cutting begins under the house. Beneath the joists to be cut, place the supports 2 feet back from the planned opening on each side. Build the temporary support system as shown with 4-by-4 beams wedged tightly in place and toenailed together. Toenail the beams to the floor joists.

You are now ready to cut the joists. Make the cuts on each side 3 inches wider than the actual opening. This allows room for the doubled joists on each side of the opening. Snap chalklines along the bottoms of the joists to be cut. Make the cuts with a saber saw or reciprocal saw, then finish up with a hand saw. The rim joist along the foundation wall will have to be drilled first so a saw blade can be inserted. When the cuts are complete, pry the joists loose from the subfloor; use nippers to cut the nails flush.

The alcove joists should be spaced the same as the existing floor joists, which is usually 16 inches on center. Support the alcove joists on the reinforced joist with joist hangers. To install the alcove joists, first place a support joist at each side of the opening and nail it to the ends of the cut floor joists. Face-nail a second joist to the first one to make a double joist. Space and hang the intervening joists. Remove the support system. Now you can start framing the alcove.

**Framing the Alcove.** To make the alcove subfloor, place the bay window on a sheet of ¾-inch exterior plywood and mark the window frame outline on it. Cut the plywood on these lines, then use it as a pattern to cut another one.

Place one of the cut plywood pieces on top of the alcove studs, align it in the opening and against the existing subfloor, then trace its outline on top of the joists. Remove the plywood and place a straight length of 2-by lumber on the *inside* of the lines and mark. Cut the joists on this inside mark. This will allow room for the rim joist to be nailed to the joist ends and still be flush with the plywood edge.

Cut the ends of the rim joist material (which is the same stock as the joists) at an angle matching the bay window (usually 45 degrees)

for a smooth fit. Nail the rim joist to the ends of the alcove joists.

Nail one piece of plywood to the bottom of the alcove joists, place insulation between the joists, and nail on the subfloor.

Now lay out and construct the cripple or knee wall around the perimeter of the alcove in a manner similar to framing the rough window or door opening described on pages 8–9. Cut the plates where the side walls join with the front walls at angles matching the window. Put the front wall in position first, then nail the two side walls to it and to the trimmer studs in the rough opening.

Finally, insert the bay window in the opening as described on page 68. Trim out the interior and install a seat across the alcove to complete the job. For more helpful ideas here, see Ortho's books, *Finish Carpentry Techniques* and *How to Design & Build Storage Projects.*

**Supporting perpendicular joists before cutting**

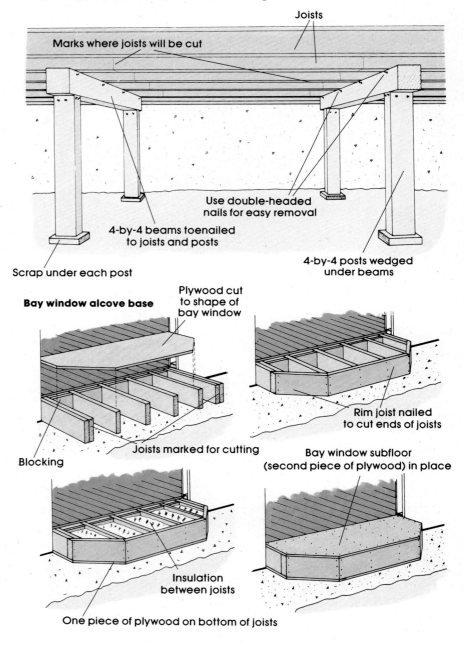

Joists

Marks where joists will be cut

Use double-headed nails for easy removal

4-by-4 beams toenailed to joists and posts

4-by-4 posts wedged under beams

Scrap under each post

**Bay window alcove base**

Plywood cut to shape of bay window

Blocking

Joists marked for cutting

Rim joist nailed to cut ends of joists

Bay window subfloor (second piece of plywood) in place

Insulation between joists

One piece of plywood on bottom of joists

# MAINTENANCE & REPAIR

Thinking of doors and windows as openings
in the weatherproofed exterior of your home points up
the importance of keeping them well sealed,
tight-fitting, and in good working order.
This chapter on door and window upkeep includes
a special section on weatherstripping and caulking.

House openings need to be functional, airtight, and beautiful. This chapter will help ensure that your doors and windows meet these requirements.

The most important aspect of doors and windows is that they function properly. Windows must admit sufficient light, and both doors and windows should operate smoothly. If they don't, but instead stick or bind, it is not only an inconvenience to you but damaging to the door or window. Forcing open a stuck door, for instance, can splinter the edge, loosen hinges, and damage the jamb. Pages 82–91 will help you repair such problems.

Hand in hand with smoothly functioning house openings is the degree of airtightness in your house. When a door or window sticks, it is usually because it is out of line, which means that while it is sticking on one side, a gap has opened on the other. Making the repair can solve two problems at once.

An airtight house also means a more energy-efficient house, and that results in lower heating and cooling costs. The quality of airtightness depends on two factors:

In a well-cared-for home, the doors and windows work as well as they look. At left, symmetry shapes a beach house. The rectangular windows in the view wall, reminiscent of a cubist painting, are topped by quarter-rounds above the bedroom windows. The rounded shape follows the curve of a barrel-vaulted ceiling and is repeated in a large arched headboard on the bed.

how well you have sealed the house, and how much you are impeding heat transference. If you have felt what seems to be a draft when standing near a single-pane window on a cold day, you've experienced heat transference: the room heat is moving past you through the window glass. A single-pane window can permit many times the heat loss of an insulated wall. Storm windows, or double-pane windows with a sealed dead-air space, provide an efficient thermal barrier to markedly reduce that heat loss.

The other major source of heat loss in a house is cracks around the doors and windows that permit actual drafts, not heat transference. A ¼-inch crack under a front door is a veritable heat exchanger, exchanging cold outside air for warm inside air. All this can cost you an astonishing amount of money. Even in a moderately sealed house, 15 percent of your fuel bill is probably being wasted; in a poorly sealed house it could be twice that or more.

By investing the amount of money you spend in about two weeks on a winter fuel bill and a few hours of your labor, you can markedly reduce your heat loss. Pages 74–81 will guide you in improving your house's airtightness.

And finally, there is no reason those doors and windows can't be beautiful as well as functional and airtight. Doors and windows that are worn can be stripped and repainted or restained. The tips on pages 92–93 will help in preparing surfaces and doing the actual painting. You can not only make doors and windows attractive again, but also prolong their life by protecting them.

## Reducing Heat Loss Through Windows

The windows in newer homes are often made with dual glass, which is the prime method of reducing heat loss through windows. If you wish to solve heat-loss problems by installing dual glass, you will have to replace the whole window; turn to pages 52–60 for instructions. If, however, you're not ready to replace single-pane windows, there are some other approaches.

### Storm Windows

Storm windows work by creating a dead-air space, just as thermal windows do. For storm windows to work efficiently, there must be no gaps between window frames and wall coverings, but there must be weep holes in the storm-window frame to release condensation.

What type of storm window you use will depend in part on the type of window you have. For instance, some sliding aluminum-framed windows have interchangeable screens or storm windows that slip into channels around the outside of the window. Others can be made up to your window sizes at custom window shops to fit directly over your existing windows. They have weatherstripping around the interior edges and are simply screwed or snapped into place.

Storm doors should be made up in custom shops to fit your door opening exactly, for if there are air leaks around the edges, much of their energy-saving value is lost.

### Plastic Sheeting

A less attractive but cheaper style of storm window can be made by simply stretching sheets of polyethylene across the outside of your windows. It is available in various sized rolls at most hardware stores. However, this material is not clear like glass, and visibility will be reduced, so it's suitable only for windows where the view is secondary.

To cover the windows, cut 4-mil or 6-mil plastic sheeting so it is 2 inches larger than the exterior window frame. Fold under 1 inch and staple the doubled edge to the top of the window frame. Cover the plastic with a length of lath cut to fit; tack in place. Repeat the process for the bottom and then the sides, covering each with lath. Run a bead of caulking around the outside of the lath to seal it.

To cover windows that you wish to see out of, there is a new window insulation kit. Working on the inside of the window, you simply tape the plastic up around the window frame, then go over it with an electric hair dryer. The heat shrinks the plastic to a wrinkle-free, clear covering. One package has enough material to cover five 3-foot by 5-foot windows.

You also can screw a sheet of acrylic plastic over the window (see illustration below).

**Plastic-film storm window**

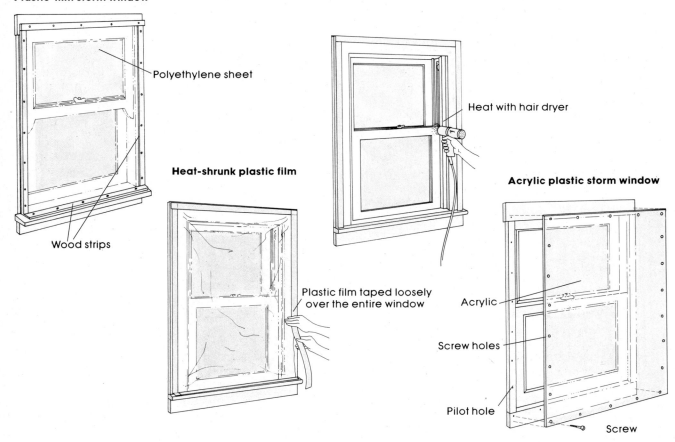

Polyethylene sheet

Wood strips

**Heat-shrunk plastic film**

Plastic film taped loosely over the entire window

Heat with hair dryer

**Acrylic plastic storm window**

Acrylic

Screw holes

Pilot hole

Screw

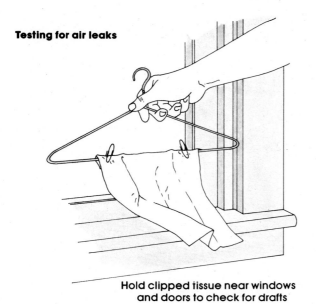

**Testing for air leaks**

Hold clipped tissue near windows and doors to check for drafts

Close a window on a dollar bill, then pull to test weatherstripping

## Reducing Heat Gain Through Windows

Windows can also bring unwanted heat into your home in the form of direct radiant heat from the sun. One way to reduce heat gain is to cover windows with a reflective film. Also on the market now are solar screens. These are placed on the outside of the windows, much like storm windows, and cut glare by 20 to 70 percent, depending on the weave of the screen. Visibility is not greatly impaired.

Some dual windows have mini-blinds set between the panes. They can be adjusted to control the amount of sunlight passing through.

And don't forget the old standby of simply hanging a bamboo or vinyl roll-up screen from the eaves.

## Filling the Gaps

You will be pleasantly surprised at the change you can bring to your house with a few hours' work at caulking and weatherstripping. Stopping air flow into the house also means a much cleaner house.

Even if you think you have a fairly airtight house, try some of these tests. On a breezy day, clip the edge of a tissue square to a hanger and then hold it at various points around the edges of doors and windows. Even faint air motions will cause it to flutter. Do the same around air conditioners, or around stove and clothes dryer vents where they pass through walls. You can also do the test with a lighted cigarette, watching the smoke movement.

Place a dollar bill across the weatherstripping of a window and then close the window. If the dollar bill comes free with little or no resistance, the weatherstripping is insufficient.

At night, have someone shine a flashlight around the edges of windows and doors. Anywhere the light penetrates, you know you have a major air leak.

Although doors and windows are primary areas of unwanted air infiltration, there are several other important parts of the house to seal off. The chart below will pinpoint them for you, with solutions suggested; for a thorough coverage of blocking these problems, see Ortho's book, *Energy-Saving Projects for the Home.*

## Stopping Air Leaks

| Problem | Solution |
| --- | --- |
| Air leak around door | Apply weatherstripping. See page 77 for choices. |
| Air leak under door | Apply rubber threshold or door sweep. |
| Air leak past exterior door frame | Apply acrylic latex caulk of matching color. |
| Air leak around window | Weatherstrip like doors. |
| Air leak around window frame | Caulk as for door frame. |
| Single-pane window | Apply 4-mil plastic inside or outside, or use thermal curtains. |

### Caulking

Caulk is a putty-like substance used to seal cracks where air might enter the house. Caulk is commonly used around the exterior trim of doors and windows to keep moisture out. It is most widely sold in standard-size cartridges but also comes in toothpaste-size dispensers for small cracks. In addition, you can buy coils of caulk for cracks ½ inch or larger. Good caulk remains elastic, depending on its quality, for three to ten years. The problem is deciding which caulking material is best for your needs.

The chart below is a guide to the basic types.

**Interiors.** Caulking around door and window frames on the inside should be done during installation. Large gaps around windows and doors should be loosely filled with insulation, and smaller gaps caulked with latex before the interior trim is put in place. If you are not sure this has been done, do not attempt to remove the interior trim boards. They are tightly nailed and you will likely split them or damage the wall. Instead, weatherstrip the window or door and caulk around the exterior trim.

**Exteriors.** Check the caulking (if there is any) where the door or window trim meets the house siding. Don't forget the trim on top. If the existing caulk is cracked, broken, or dried out, use a chisel to remove all of it. Use an acrylic latex of a matching color and apply a bead to fill all gaps.

## Caulking Materials

| Type | Advantage | Disadvantage |
| --- | --- | --- |
| Oil based | Low cost. Useful indoors where little or no expansion likely, such as behind baseboards. | Dries hard. Is porous, and wood should be primed first if in a visible area. |
| Latex, vinyl latex | Easy to use, works on damp surfaces, is paintable, inexpensive. | Lowest quality of latex caulks. For interior use only; tends to dry hard. |
| Acrylic latex | Easy to use, wide color choice, paintable, cleans up with water, provides good seal around exterior doors and windows. | Breaks up in permanently wet locations. |
| Butyl rubber | Adheres well to wood, metal, masonry. Excellent water resistance. | Considerable shrinkage, must cure one week before it can be painted. |
| Synthetic rubber | Does not need to be painted; chemical- and heat-resistant. Adheres well to wood, masonry, metal. | Considerable shrinkage; painted surfaces must be cleaned before application. |
| Polyurethane | Very elastic, resists abrasion, good for filling masonry cracks. | Requires gloves and good ventilation during application; surface must be primed before application. |
| Silicone | Remains flexible even in low temperatures, adheres well to metal, glass, masonry, can be applied at subfreezing temperatures. | Primer needed on wood and masonry surfaces; cannot be painted. Requires good ventilation during application. |
| Urethane foam | Excellent for filling large areas; provides good insulation; easy to use. | Dries hard; rough edges should be smoothed before completely dry. |

## Using a Caulking Gun

A caulking gun, available in most hardware stores for less than $5, is a must when it comes to sealing up your house. To insert the caulking cartridge, turn the handle up so the trigger does not engage the notches, and pull it all the way back. Insert the cartridge, turn the handle down, then pull the trigger a few times until the plunger lightly engages the cartridge. Trim the tip of the cartridge with a sharp knife. Small crack, small bead.

Break the inner seal with the built-in probe or a nail. Turn the cartridge tip so the caulk will be forced into the crack. Hold the gun at about a 45-degree angle.

To remove a cartridge, turn the handle up and pull all the way back. Lift the cartridge out. To seal a cartridge, insert a nail in the tip. If you are leaving the cartridge in the gun, release the pressure before storing it.

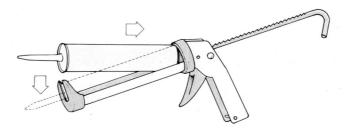

**Caulking gun and cartridge**

## Weatherstripping Materials

Weatherstripping, generally metal or a type of rubber, is used around doors and around windows that must open and shut. There are so many different types of weatherstripping on the market, you may feel defeated before you start. Here is a selection of weatherstripping materials and where to use them:

**Felt strip** Inexpensive: made of hair, wool, or polyester. Tack or glue around double-hung windows.

**Foam tape** Made of polyurethane or vinyl, it's easy to apply. Self-adhering. Use on double-hung windows or on side casing for sliding glass door.

**Sponge rubber** Made of neoprene, somewhat harder and longer lasting than either felt strip or foam tape. Use in same manner.

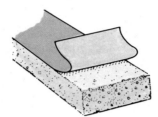

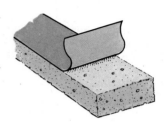

**Flange stripping** Made of vinyl or rubber. The flat part is tacked to the door or window jamb and the bulb is compressed when the unit is closed.

**Tension strip** Made of metal or vinyl, widely considered the most effective and longest lasting weatherstripping. More expensive than others. Vinyl has self-sticking surface. Metal is more difficult to install. Available in colors.

**Door sweep** Simple and effective. The metal or plastic top section is screwed to the inside of the door. Slot allows fine adjustment. The vinyl sweep will catch on a carpet but is an excellent choice over hardwood floors. Adjustable type screws to the outside of the door; spring mechanism raises it above carpet.

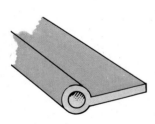

**Bristle sweep** This device with nylon bristles in a metal or plastic retainer is a good choice under sliding glass doors.

**Door shoe** This device is very effective. The metal shoe with a drip cap to block blowing rain is screwed to door's exterior and then vinyl strip is inserted. Careful trimming of the door is required for a perfect fit.

**Threshold gasket** This weatherstripping is built into the threshold instead of into the door. You will have to remove the door to screw the device to the existing threshold. The door must then be carefully measured and cut for precise fit.

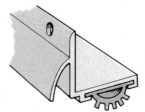

# SEALING THE HOUSE
## CONTINUED

### Weatherstripping a Door

You can weatherstrip most doors by following the same instructions as for weatherstripping a window (see pages 80–81). Although doors tend to be larger than windows, they are generally easier to weatherstrip because they lack the problems of double sashes and center bars.

Whatever method you use, first measure the stripping carefully against the frame. Then seat it onto the frame against the doorstop so that it fits tightly when the door is closed, but not so tightly that the door can't close. To ensure a proper fit, you may want to tack the stripping loosely into place first; test it by opening and closing the door gently a few times. Then you can drive your nails and set the heads.

The exterior door is a major source of air infiltration. Its opening is extremely large, and the weight of the door swinging on its hinges over many years tends to loosen screws in the hinges and to cause the door to sag, making its edges meet the jambs unevenly. So it's definitely worth your while to weatherstrip an exterior door, even though doing so may present some difficulties.

If your door hangs unevenly, you may have to remove it from its hinges and rehang it (see pages 84–85). Otherwise the seal between the door and the stripping may not be tight. You may want to take advantage of this situation to trim the door bottom to accommodate a door shoe or a threshold gasket, both extremely useful weatherstripping devices.

### Applying the Weatherstripping

Begin with the lock strip, the small piece of stripping provided with most kits. Because this piece is the same height as, and placed behind, the strike plate, it will help guide you in measuring and placing your weatherstripping on the latch side of the jamb.

When the lock strip is in place, complete the stripping on the sides and top of the jamb, keeping the flanges facing toward the door stop. The bottom of the door will be stripped in another fashion.

### Weatherstripping the Bottom of the Door

Of course, since cold air falls, it is most likely to enter your home through the lowest available cracks. Virtually any house is subject to this kind of infiltration at the bottoms of exterior doors.

There are various ways to plug these door-bottom cracks. All methods entail either lowering the bottom of the door or raising the top of the threshold over which the door passes.

The most common and effective kinds of weatherstripping you can add to the bottoms of your own doors are the door sweep, the door shoe, and the threshold gasket.

**Door Sweep.** The simplest door-bottom weatherstripping is a door sweep—vinyl or bristle—that you can attach easily while the door is still on its hinges. Just cut the sweep to size and screw it to the base of the door in a position that allows the door to open and close easily.

Adjustable door sweeps raise up when you open the door inward (over your carpeting, for example), and lower back down when you close the door, creating a tight seal. The adjustable sweep is surface-mounted to the outside face of your door. To attach it, close your door and measure the width between the stops. Using a hacksaw, cut the sweep to this size. While you cut, hold the movable part of the sweep in the "up" position; be sure not to cut the end with the plastic button. Screw the sweep to the door with the door closed; hold the sweep in the "down" position so the rubber bottom, which must be on the hinge side of the door, is pressed snugly against the threshold. Note where the plastic button hits the stop. Open the door and nail the little strike

### Weatherstripping installation

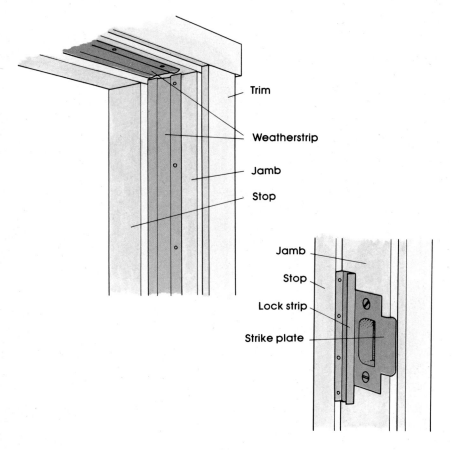

Trim

Weatherstrip

Jamb

Stop

Jamb

Stop

Lock strip

Strike plate

plate that comes with the sweep in position at this spot.

**Door Shoe.** The door shoe is similar to an adjustable door sweep, but it doesn't "sweep." Instead, the vinyl ridges of its tubular gasket make a tight seal with the door sill or threshold.

Attach a door shoe as you would an adjustable door sweep, gauging its fit as you work and trimming it with a hacksaw if necessary. Remove the curved vinyl ridge from the shoe, slide the shoe over the door bottom, screw it on securely, and replace the vinyl so that it makes a tight seal with your threshold.

**Threshold Gasket.** If you intend to attach a door shoe, your threshold must be in fairly good condition, and preferably made of wood, so that the ridges of the gasket can grasp and make a tight seal. If you have no threshold, or if yours is worn enough to be replaced, you might consider installing a threshold gasket, as well as door-bottom weatherstripping. The disadvantage of a threshold gasket is that it gets walked on and eventually wears out.

To attach any threshold, it is often necessary to remove the door from its hinges in order to gain complete access to the threshold area. You may also have to trim the bottom of the door to accommodate the added height of the threshold. If so, first be sure to measure your sill, door bottom, and new threshold carefully, so that you know exactly how much of which part you must trim. If you trim too much from your door bottom, you will defeat the purpose of weatherstripping it; if you do not trim enough, your new gasket will wear out very quickly.

If you must trim the door, do it before you trim the threshold. Then cut the threshold to the proper width with a hacksaw, and file it smooth. Center your threshold, and screw it into place.

In any case, to achieve a tight seal, you may have to remove the door and bevel its base about ⅛ inch against the vinyl. Do not bevel in the wrong direction, or you may find it impossible to open your door.

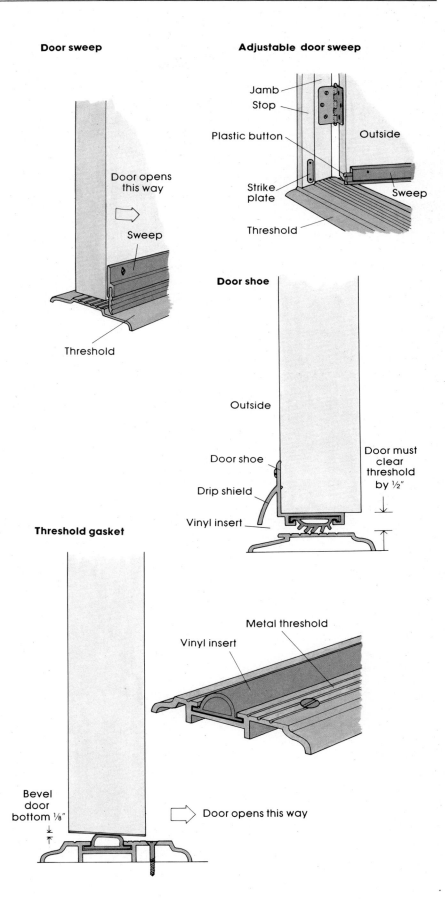

**Door sweep**

Door opens this way

Sweep

Threshold

**Adjustable door sweep**

Jamb

Stop

Plastic button

Outside

Strike plate

Sweep

Threshold

**Door shoe**

Outside

Door shoe

Drip shield

Vinyl insert

Door must clear threshold by ½"

**Threshold gasket**

Metal threshold

Vinyl insert

Bevel door bottom ⅛"

Door opens this way

## Weatherstripping a Window

Every window, like every kind of stripping, has its own peculiarities, so use these instructions as general guidelines, and follow the instructions thoughtfully provided by the manufacturer of the weatherstripping you select.

Weatherstripping is only appropriate for windows that open. Fixed-pane and greenhouse windows and skylights should be caulked and do not require weatherstripping; jalousie windows cannot be fully sealed, so they are recommended for warm climates or for porches attached to properly sealed houses.

The combination of the double-hung sash and metal tension stripping shown here allows for the most complete explanation of the procedure of weatherstripping a window. As with any weatherstripping, metal strips should be installed with the resilient face pressing against the sash tightly enough to make a good seal but not so tightly that your window will stick.

## Double-Hung Window

Measure strips to fit the side channels for both sashes, the upper rail of the top sash, the lower rail of the bottom sash, and the lower rail of the top sash (the center bar). Cut the strips with tin snips.

Slide the side-channel strips into place between the sashes and jambs and nail them in place. Be careful that you do not cover the mechanisms in the upper parts of the channels.

Slide the upper-rail top-sash strip into the window's top channel and the lower-rail bottom-sash strip into the window's bottom channel; nail in place. Or you can nail the upper-rail top-sash strip to the top of the upper sash, and nail the lower-rail bottom-sash strip to the underside of the bottom sash.

Nail your last strip to the inside of the lower rail of the top sash (the center bar). If the strips don't fit tightly enough, you can pry out the side-channel flanges with a screwdriver or a putty knife. Set all nails to prevent snagging.

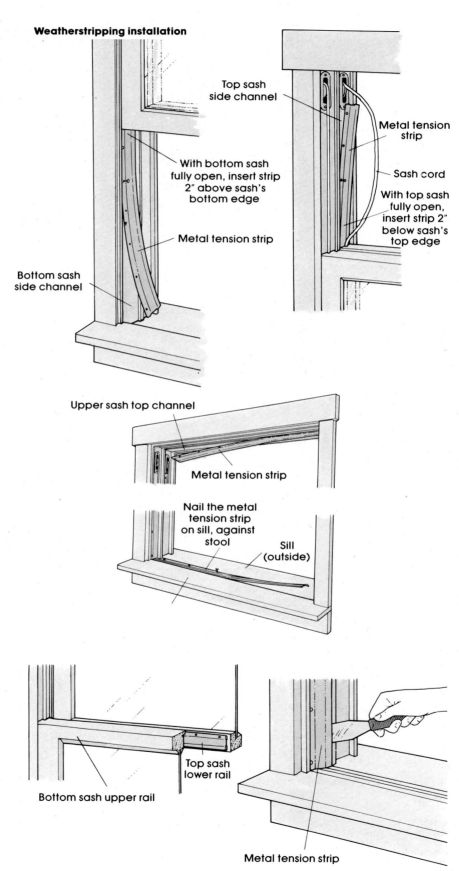

**Weatherstripping installation**

Top sash side channel

Metal tension strip

Sash cord

With bottom sash fully open, insert strip 2" above sash's bottom edge

With top sash fully open, insert strip 2" below sash's top edge

Metal tension strip

Bottom sash side channel

Upper sash top channel

Metal tension strip

Nail the metal tension strip on sill, against stool

Sill (outside)

Bottom sash upper rail

Top sash lower rail

Metal tension strip

## Sliding Window

Weatherstripping a sliding window is the same as doing a double-hung sash window—just imagine it's lying on its side. If only one sash slides, use metal tension stripping in the channel that opens, and seal the three remaining edges of the movable sash with tubular flange stripping to create a good seal all around the sliding sash.

## Casement Window

For a wooden casement window or any kind of tilting window such as rotating, awning, or hopper, nail the weatherstripping to the frame with the flange along the edge toward which the window opens. For a metal casement window, buy a deeply grooved gasket stripping that can be fitted over all the metal edges of the window frame (available at most hardware stores). To make this stripping hold better, first apply a rubber/metal or a vinyl/metal glue to the frame edge or the gasket channel.

## Alternate Methods

Different types of weatherstripping require varied installation methods. Some of those variations are:

**Flange Stripping.** Vinyl or rubber stripping can simply be tacked all around the sash. If you nail it to the outside of the window frame, it will be less visible, but inside or out, it should fit tightly all around, including the lower rail of the top sash. Nail gasket stripping to the window frame with the thick or bulbous side against the sash. Make sure that the rolled edges fit tightly against the window when it's closed. Then add stripping to the lower rail of the top sash (the center bar) on the inside edge, to make a tight seal between the sashes when the whole window is closed. Make sure to strip all edges of the window.

**Foam Tape and Sponge Rubber.** Foam tape or any other adhesive-backed stripping may be simply pressed into place with your fingers. Clean the surface so the tape can adhere. Then apply the stripping, slowly pulling the paper or plastic backing off the tape as you go. Do not use this type of weather-stripping where it will encounter friction, such as in side channels—it will wear out quickly, or even pull right off.

**Felt Stripping.** To install felt stripping, you can either staple it in place with an ordinary heavy-duty stapler, or you can nail the felt to the window frame, as with gasket strip-ping. Also add a length of felt to the inside of the lower rail of the top sash, to block infiltration between the sashes. However, you should not attach felt stripping to the outside of a window where it is liable to get wet because it may rot. As with foam tape, do not use felt stripping where it will encounter friction.

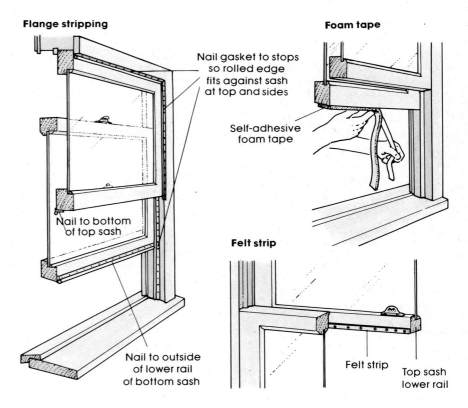

**Wood casement window**

Flange toward open window

Sill

Stool (inside)

**Metal casement window**

Grooved strip over metal edge

Stool (inside)

**Flange stripping**

Nail gasket to stops so rolled edge fits against sash at top and sides

Nail to bottom of top sash

Nail to outside of lower rail of bottom sash

**Foam tape**

Self-adhesive foam tape

**Felt strip**

Felt strip

Top sash lower rail

## Replacing Broken Glass

### Wood-framed Windows

**Sash Window.** Remove the shards from the sash, wearing gloves to protect yourself.

Next, remove the putty by scraping with a putty knife. If the putty is too hard, soften it with a soldering iron. Pull out all the glazier's points and then scrape and sand the old wood. Now coat the bare wood with a sealer or linseed oil to keep the wood from drawing the oil from the new putty or the glazing compound.

The simplest way to get a new pane of glass is to carefully measure the window opening and ask a glazier to cut a replacement piece for you. Have the new pane of glass cut ⅛ inch smaller in both dimensions than the window opening.

On the outside, spread a thin layer—about ⅛ inch—of glazing compound on the edge of the opening and then insert the glass pane. Do not press so hard that you cause the cushion layer of compound to squeeze out around the glass.

Next, tap the glazier's points in place around the window on the outside. Space them about 6 inches apart. Drive them in halfway with a hammer and screwdriver.

Roll the final layer of glazing compound into a rope about ½ inch or less thick, and press it into place with your fingers over the glazier's points. With your putty knife, press the rope in further and leave a smooth, beveled bead, starting at one corner and moving to the next in one continuous stroke. The bead should extend to the outer edge of the sash and be as high as the sash edge on the inside of the glass.

Clean the glass. When the putty or compound is dry enough to touch without leaving a fingerprint, repaint it. Let the paint lap onto the glass about 1/16 inch as an added seal.

**Fixed-pane Window.** Remove the outside stops and the broken glass. To insert new glass, follow the instructions for installing a fixed-pane window (pages 54–57).

A safety note: If the window is in a high-risk area and has been broken before, use clear acrylic or tempered glass.

### Aluminum-framed Windows

**Casement Window.** Casement window panes are replaced in much the same manner as for wooden frames. However, you will find that instead of glazier's points, the panes are held with small spring clips inserted in holes in the frame.

After the putty has been completely removed, sand the edges and repaint to prevent corrosion. Replace the windowpane as outlined above, using the spring clips instead of glazier's points.

Some varieties of casement windows use metal strips to hold the panes in place. Before screwing these back in place, check that the rubber gasket has not been damaged. If it has, replace it.

**Sliding Window.** To remove broken glass from sliding windows, the sash must be taken apart, usually by removing screws. The glass is held in place by a rubber gasket. After this has been pulled out and all glass particles removed, reinstall the glass and gasket, and reassemble the sash.

### Storm Windows

If the window has a wood frame, replace the glass as described for a wood-framed sash window, above; if it has a metal frame, refer to the instructions for sliding aluminum-framed windows.

### Doors

To replace broken glass in a door, see the appropriate window section above, depending on what the framing material is. If you have broken sliding glass doors, consult a glass and window supply firm.

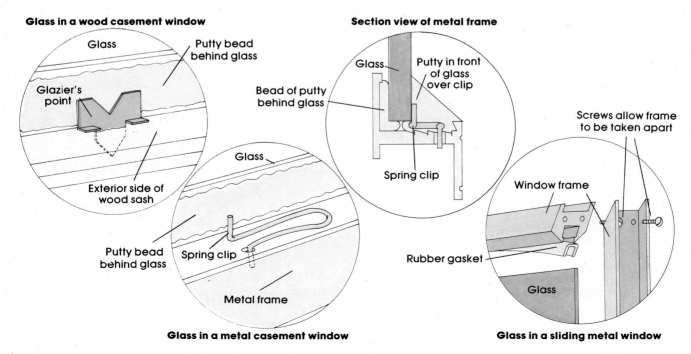

**Glass in a wood casement window**

Glass

Putty bead behind glass

Glazier's point

Exterior side of wood sash

Putty bead behind glass

**Glass in a metal casement window**

Spring clip

Glass

Metal frame

**Section view of metal frame**

Glass

Putty in front of glass over clip

Bead of putty behind glass

Spring clip

Screws allow frame to be taken apart

Window frame

Rubber gasket

Glass

**Glass in a sliding metal window**

## Repairing Damaged Screening

What appears to be a small hole is sometimes actually just the screen wires spread apart. Use a nail or awl to realign them.

**Wire.** For small tears in wire screens, either buy a ready-made patch or make your own from matching screening. For your own patch, cut a square of screen about twice the size of the hole, then unravel all four sides a little. Bend these individual wires at a right angle, push the patch over the hole, and bend the wires back.

**Plastic.** For plastic screens, the method used for wire screens won't work. On very small holes, align the broken ends and bond them with epoxy resin. On a larger tear, overlay slightly with a matching piece of screen and glue it in place with epoxy resin. Line up each strand for a smooth job.

## Replacing Screening

**Wood Frames.** With wood frames, first pry up the molding that holds the screen in place. Work slowly so you don't split it. Remove the screen and staples.

Cut the new screen 1 inch larger than the opening, then staple the bottom edge in place. To stretch the screen, use either of the methods illustrated here. Staple the top while the screen is stretched, then release the tension and do the sides. Trim the edges with a utility knife and then replace the molding.

**Aluminum Frames.** To replace screens on aluminum frames, use a screwdriver to pry up one corner of the metal or plastic spline that holds the screen in a channel. Work your way around the door. Cut the new screen 1 inch larger than the opening, then press it into the channels with the special roller tool designed for this, available at hardware stores. Replace the spline as you work your way around the door. The combination of the tool and the spline that compresses into the channel will pull the screen tight. Trim off the excess using either tin snips or a utility knife.

**Fixing a hole in wire screening**

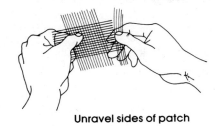

Unravel sides of patch

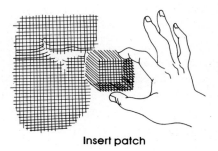

Insert patch

**Stretching screening on a wood frame**

**Method 1, using clamps and boards**

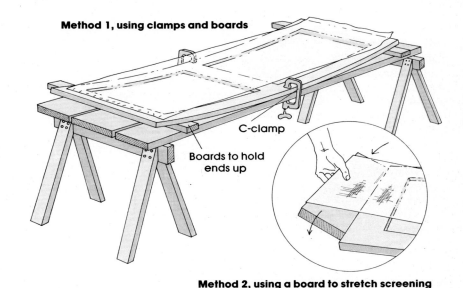

C-clamp

Boards to hold ends up

**Method 2, using a board to stretch screening**

**Replacing screening in an aluminum door**

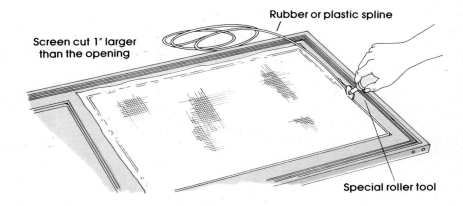

Rubber or plastic spline

Screen cut 1" larger than the opening

Special roller tool

# SOLVING DOOR PROBLEMS

Sometimes, despite your best efforts, a door refuses to fit. It may be because the jamb is out of kilter, the house has settled, hinges are worn, or the door is warped. And sometimes a new door must be trimmed down to fit an existing entranceway.

One tends to get used to living with a door that doesn't work right, because it seems a lot of trouble to fix. But fixing such doors should be high on your priority list, because of the damage a misaligned door can cause to the door and jamb, and the high amount of air infiltration that occurs around it. Here are some of the most common door problems and what to do about them.

## Fixing a Door That Doesn't Fit

**Coping with Swollen Wood.** A wood door may not quite fit during a wet or humid period because moisture makes it swell. Planing it down to fit during the wet weather often means it will be loose during the dry season when it shrinks back to normal. You will have to judge if the sticking is bad enough to justify that. For just a slight binding, soaping the area will probably help. The real solution to swollen wood is to take the door down, strip all paint off, seal it properly, and stain or paint it again.

**Fixing Hinges.** If the door tends to stick year around, the first area to investigate is the hinges. Open the door and check that all the screws are tight. If one or more are loose and won't tighten down, the wood behind has been stripped by the screw threads. An easy and effective solution is to remove the screw, coat a wooden match with glue, and push into the hole. When it is dry, it will provide ample filler to reset the screw.

If the door sticks and the hinges are all tight, stand back and study the closed door. If it is hanging crooked you will be able to see the variations in the gaps on the latch side. Wherever the gap is wider—at top or bottom—shim that hinge out to straighten the door. Loosen the leaf of the hinge on the jamb, cut a piece of cardboard the height of the butt hinge and about ¼ inch wide, slip it behind the leaf, and retighten the screws.

There is some trial and error in such shimming, and this can be eliminated by correcting the hinge another way. Remove the pin and then shim between door and threshold until the door is straight in the jamb. Now take a large wrench or a pair of smooth-jawed pliers and bend the knuckles of the hinge leaf attached to the jamb until they

**Shimming a hinge**

Shim the whole hinge to move the door slightly away from the jamb

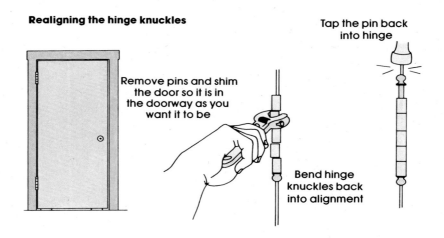

**Realigning the hinge knuckles**

Remove pins and shim the door so it is in the doorway as you want it to be

Bend hinge knuckles back into alignment

Tap the pin back into hinge

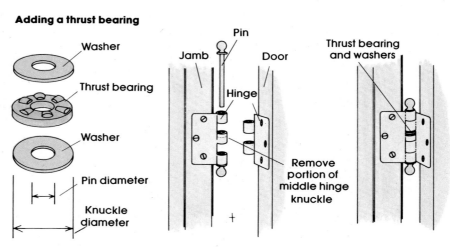

**Adding a thrust bearing**

Washer

Thrust bearing

Washer

Pin diameter

Knuckle diameter

Pin

Jamb

Door

Hinge

Thrust bearing and washers

Remove portion of middle hinge knuckle

are aligned with those on the door. Reinsert the pin. You should be able to realign the door about ⅛ inch without binding any other hinges.

Butt hinges on heavy exterior doors eventually wear, allowing the door to sag. A careful look at your hinges will reveal if this is your problem. If it is, or if you are installing a big custom-made door, use this tip: add a thrust bearing, available at bearing-supply stores, to the center hinge. Thrust bearings, which come in a variety of sizes, have a series of hardened rollers built into them. Use a bearing washer on each side of the bearing and install as illustrated, in place of a portion of the middle knuckle on the jamb leaf; cut it away with a hacksaw.

**Planing and Cutting.** A sticking wooden door can often be fixed with just a little sanding or planing. Sanding is slower but more accurate when only a little wood must be removed. Wrap the sandpaper around a block of wood to keep it flat on the door edge. And remember that whenever a door is sanded, planed, or cut, it must be resealed and stained or painted.

The first problem is finding just where a door sticks. If you can't see it, slip a piece of paper in the closed door around the suspect area; wherever the paper can't be pulled out, the door is binding.

To work on the door, remove it from its hinges, bottom hinge first. If you don't have a helper or a door buck (see page 27) to hold the door, you can put one end in a corner of the room to brace it. When planing the edges of a door, always work with the grain, or you will gouge the wood. When planing the top or bottom of a door, work from the outer edges toward the center. Planing from the center to the edge will most certainly result in splitting a large chunk out of the stile edge. When you finish, lay a straightedge on the door and sight along it for any irregularities. These may be corrected by sanding.

When a door must be cut to fit an opening or to clear a new threshold, there are three key points to keep in mind: the cut must be perfectly straight, you must not leave a ragged saw edge, and hollow-core doors cannot be trimmed more than 1 inch.

Cutting freehand with a circular saw is too inaccurate for a door. First draw a line where you want the cut, then clamp a straight board on the door to guide the saw. The factory edge of a piece of plywood is good for this. Position the saw carefully on the line at one end, then clamp the guide into position.

Measure from the line to the guide and then set the far end of the guide the same distance.

For smooth cuts, use a carbide-tipped plywood sawblade. Even this fine-toothed blade will not prevent hollow-core veneer doors from splintering. The door must be first scored with a utility knife on the cutting line. Carry the cutting line clear around the door; then—using a straightedge guide—score the line. This severs the surface fibers and the result is a smooth edge when the door is cut.

If you have many doors to do, the saw jig illustrated here will be a great time saver. Make the jig about 7 feet long and 12 inches wide out of a piece of ¼-inch-thick hardboard or plywood. Glue and screw a perfectly straight piece of 2-inch-wide hardboard or plywood down the center. Use a square to double-check that your saw blade is set at a 90-degree angle. Set the saw against the guide and cut down one side of the jig. Set the saw at a 5-degree angle, which is the amount exterior doors are trimmed on the inner edge to clear door jambs, and cut down the other side. Mark each side clearly. To cut any door, just clamp the jig along the line and, using it as a guide, run your saw along the edge.

**Sawing a door**

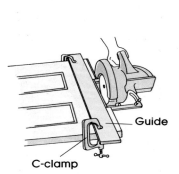

Guide

C-clamp

**Door sawing jig**

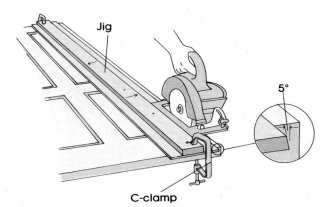

Jig

5°

C-clamp

**Bowed door**

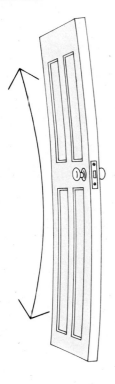

**Warped door**

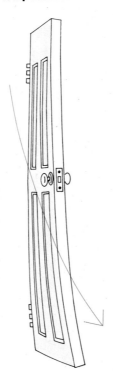

**Straightening a warped door**

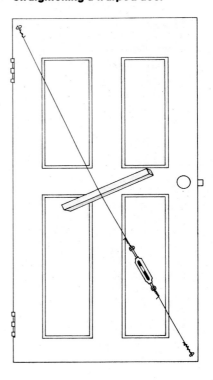

**Repositioning a door stop**

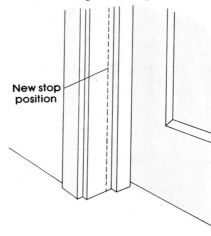

New stop position

### Fixing a Warped Door

**Straightening the Door.** A good door often becomes nearly unserviceable because it is warped or bowed. Rather than throwing it away, try straightening it.

If the door is simply bowed in the middle, you may be able to straighten it with weights. Set it on a pair of sawhorses or chairs, with the bulge up, and place weights—books or bricks or whatever—in the center until the weight straightens the door.

If the door is twisted, it must be pulled back into line. This is done with a couple lengths of wire and a turnbuckle, available at hardware stores. First, put two screw hooks at the diagonal corners of the warp. Attach the wires to the screw hooks and the turnbuckle, then tighten. The wire should stretch over a short length of 2 by 4 on edge in the center to provide more leverage. Increase tension daily over a period of three or four days. Tightening all at once may pull the screw hooks out.

**Moving Door Stops.** When a door is just slightly out of line and you don't want to try straightening it, you may be able to simply move the door stops to conform with the door. Tap a flat trowel down the edge of the stop on both sides. If it is not set into, or part of, the jamb, you'll be able to gently pry it loose. Close the door, then move the stop to the proper position on the door, and nail. That twisted door should now look quite respectable.

### Replacing a Threshold

Thresholds are normally made of hardwood and will take years of wear. But eventually they will show their age and must be replaced.

First, inspect the threshold to see if it is flush against the door jambs or extends under them. If you have the first situation, removal is simple. Just take off the door stops,

**Installing a new threshold**

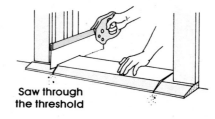

Saw through the threshold

then use a crow bar to pry the threshold up.

Generally, however, the threshold extends under the jambs. In this case, saw through the threshold on each side of the jambs next to the stops, which can be left in place. Pry up the center piece and use a hammer and chisel to knock out the end pieces under the jambs. Do as little damage as possible to the pieces so they can be used as a pattern for cutting the new threshold. If the old threshold was too badly damaged to use, measure the opening carefully and cut a cardboard pattern to fit.

When tapping the new threshold into place, use a hammer with a protective block of wood. Don't force the threshold, or you may split the jamb. Instead, plane or sand the edges that fit under the jamb. If one end is low, shim it with strips of roofing felt. Once you have a good fit, remove the threshold and lay three thick beads of caulk on the subfloor to seal out drafts.

Since hardwood splits easily, nail holes should be drilled first. Make the holes about half the diameter of the nails. Better yet, predrill the threshold to accept countersunk screws. Tighten the screws and fill the holes with wood putty.

## Fixing a Hole in a Hollow-Core Door

Hollow-core doors are easily damaged, but fortunately they are also easy to repair.

The first step is to pull away splintered wood around the break and lightly sand around the hole to remove any rough edges. Next, ball up a sheet of newspaper, coat the back of it with glue, and push it into the hole. Use a wide putty knife to cover the paper with a layer of spackling compound. This is a fast-setting repair material for holes in such places as floors and walls. It is a powder that is simply mixed with water. Let the first coat dry overnight, then apply the second coat, bringing it out flush with the door surface. If you try to fill the hole with just one thick layer, it will shrink too much as it dries. When the repair is completely dry, sand it smooth and repaint the entire door.

**Installing a new threshold**

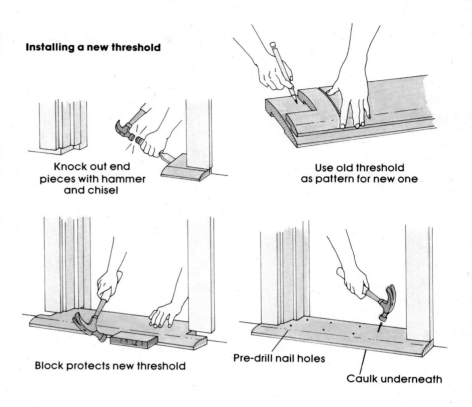

Knock out end pieces with hammer and chisel

Use old threshold as pattern for new one

Block protects new threshold

Pre-drill nail holes

Caulk underneath

**Hollow-core door repair**

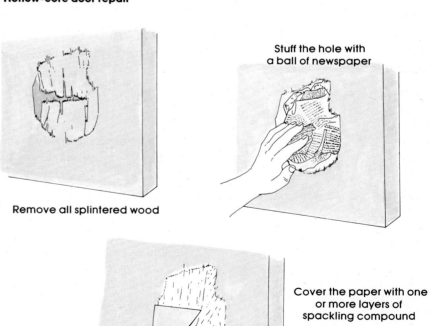

Remove all splintered wood

Stuff the hole with a ball of newspaper

Cover the paper with one or more layers of spackling compound

**Splintered door repair**

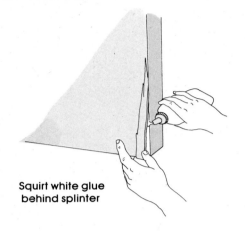

Squirt white glue
behind splinter

**Strengthening a screen door**

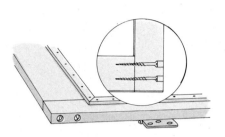

Countersink long wood screws
through the stiles into
the ends of the rails

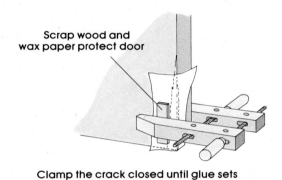

Scrap wood and
wax paper protect door

Clamp the crack closed until glue sets

T-brace
Turnbuckle
Run light wire in a figure 8
through turnbuckle

### Fixing a Splintered Door

The bottom or top edge of a wooden door, particularly a veneer hollow-core door, may become splintered along one edge where it fits too tightly in the door frame.

Remove the door if necessary, then squirt some white glue under the splintered area. Push the veneer in and wipe off the excess glue. Place a piece of wax paper over the glued area and then apply a clamp. Use scrap wood under the clamp jaws to protect the door.

If a piece of wood is missing from a door, fill the hole with wood putty. If the crack is more than 1/8 inch deep, fill to half its depth, let dry overnight, and then smooth in a top layer. Sand when dry and paint or stain to match the door.

### Fixing a Dent in a Metal Door

Although metal doors are quite durable, they can be dented by a sharp blow. For repairs on your particular door, consult with your dealer or the manufacturer.

However, one standard way of fixing dents is to sand the area down to bare metal and then use a putty knife to smooth in plastic filler used to repair dents in car bodies. Small cans are available in any automotive store. Sand the filler smooth when dry and paint to match the door.

### Fixing a Bent Sliding-Door Rail

A bent rail in a sliding glass door is an uncommon occurrence, but it may happen. If the irregularity is small, bend the rail back into line with a pair of pliers. For longer misalignments—2 or more inches—place a block of 2 by 4 against the bowed-out section of rail and hammer the wood block until the rail is brought back into line.

### Fixing a Sagging Screen Door

Screen doors often sag because they come apart at the joints. A proper way to fix this is to pry the joint apart slightly, fill it with glue, and clamp it. Then drill through the edge of the stile into the end of the rails and tighten with screws.

If the door still sags, attach two T-braces as shown and connect with a light steel cable. Use a turnbuckle near one corner to pull the wire tight and keep it that way.

# TREATING WINDOW PAINS

### Eliminating Window Sticking

**Double-Hung Window.** Of the many varieties of windows available, the centuries-old double-hung style is most prone to trouble, particularly sticking. There are two basic reasons for this: dirt or paint has worked into the channels, or the window and frame have swollen in damp weather.

If the window simply won't open, start the repair by working a stiff putty knife (not a screwdriver, which will gouge the sash) around the window between the sash and stops. Do it both inside and outside, breaking away any paint that may have sealed the window shut. Use a hammer to tap the putty knife in firmly, and work it back and forth to loosen the window.

If the window still will not move, tap a hatchet blade or metal wedge between the bottom of the sash and the sill from the outside. Work slowly across the base of the window so the sash moves upward evenly and doesn't bind.

Once you have opened the window, scrape away any loose paint and clean the pulley stiles, or window channels, thoroughly. This area can be lubricated with a silicone spray, paraffin, or wax.

If the window still doesn't move freely, it may be that the wood in the window and the stops has swollen, causing a bind. One way to correct this is to cut a 6-inch length of wood that fits snugly in the channel. Hammer it into the channel at various points to widen the channel slightly. The inside and outside stops should spread enough to let the sash move freely.

If all of this still doesn't result in a smoothly operating window, the stops and both sashes will have to be removed. For details on that process, see page 90. Once the sashes have been removed, sand or plane both sides evenly until the window moves freely.

**Sliding Window.** When one of these sticks, first see if it has been painted shut. If so, run a putty knife around the edge of the sash to break the bond, as described for the double-hung window.

More likely, the sticking is caused by debris in the tracks at the bottom. Vacuum the area clean and then lubricate with paraffin or a silicone spray.

Don't try to pry the window loose with a screwdriver or other such tool. You're more likely to bend the tracks permanently out of line than to stop the sticking.

**Casement Window.** As with other window types, check first to see if the window has been painted shut. If so, clear it with a putty knife worked between the sash and the frame, as described for the double-hung window.

The most common problem with casements is a stiff adjusting arm. See page 91 for instructions on dealing with this problem.

**Freeing a stuck window**

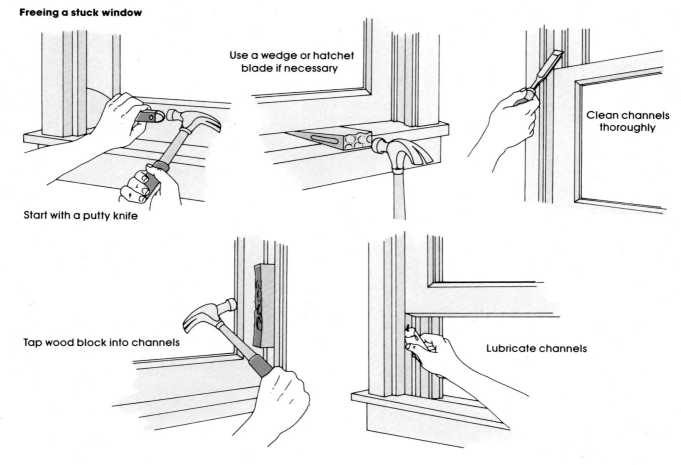

Start with a putty knife

Use a wedge or hatchet blade if necessary

Clean channels thoroughly

Tap wood block into channels

Lubricate channels

## Repairing a Window

### Double-Hung Window

**Replacing a Sash Cord.** Start by removing the stop along the side that has the broken or tangled sash cord. It may be screwed in place. If it is not, pry it loose with a chisel or flat pry bar, working from inside the channel if possible to minimize damage.

Once the stop molding on the lower sash has been removed, ease the sash out of the frame just enough to free the knotted end of the cord from the sash groove. Lower the weight gently and let the knot rest against the pulley.

To get at the weight, there may be a small access panel at the bottom of the channel. If it has never been removed, you may not be able to see it under the paint. Search out the panel with a nail or awl, then find the one or two nails or screws that are holding it in place. In very old homes this panel may never have been cut completely through and you will have to finish the job, using a drill and a keyhole saw. If there is no access panel, you will have to remove the side of the window casing to reach the weight.

Note that even if it is the upper sash cord that needs repair, you still must first remove the lower sash. To remove the upper sash you must next remove the parting strip that separates the two sashes. Slide the upper window down as far as it will go. Then, working from the top, begin removing the parting strip. It is usually set in a groove and can be pulled free with a pair of pliers, but sometimes it has been screwed or nailed in place, so check before pulling.

Use protective pieces of wood on each side of the parting strip so it is not chewed by the pliers. The upper sash cord and weight are removed in the same manner as for the lower one.

If the window has sash cords, you should take this opportunity to replace them with chains so as to minimize future maintenance problems. Drop the chain down the channel and then run it through the hole at the top of the weight. Secure the weight to the chain with wire.

Now, put the sash back in its approximate place, as if it were closed, and raise the weight until it is just below the sash pulley. Fasten the chain securely to the sash by inserting two screws through the links. Make sure the screw heads do not protrude beyond the slot.

For the upper window, the sash should be all the way up and the weights about 2 inches from the bottom of the window opening.

Before reinstalling the panel cover and stops, make sure the windows work smoothly.

**Double-hung window repair**

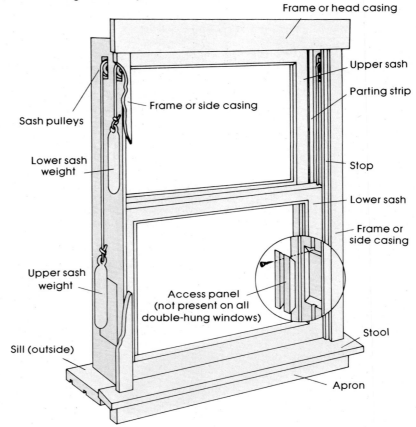

Frame or head casing

Upper sash

Parting strip

Frame or side casing

Sash pulleys

Lower sash weight

Stop

Lower sash

Frame or side casing

Upper sash weight

Access panel (not present on all double-hung windows)

Stool

Sill (outside)

Apron

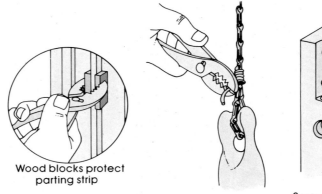

Wood blocks protect parting strip

Wire chain to the weights

Screw chain to the sash in the cord slot

## Sash spring lift

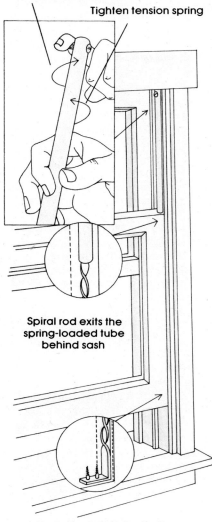

Loosen tension spring

Tighten tension spring

Spiral rod exits the spring-loaded tube behind sash

Rod attaches to the bottom of the sash with screws

**Adjusting a Spring Lift.** You can spot this device by the metal tube that runs up the window casing channel. It eliminates the need for sash cords and weights, and it can be tightened or loosened to adjust the window movement.

If the window tends to creep up after opening, the spring is too tight. To loosen it, remove the tube at the top of the window and let the screw unwind two or three turns to the left. Keep firm control of the screw. If the window does not move easily, give the screw a couple of turns to the right to increase the tension.

**Replacing a Spring Balance.** This device can be easily installed to replace the sash cords and weights. Built something like a self-retracting steel measuring tape, it is designed to fit into the opening for the pulleys on a double-hung window frame. An adapter hooks the tape to the sash. Sash balances come in different sizes for different size windows. A chart that accompanies the kit will tell you what size is most appropriate.

## Casement Window

Wooden windows are usually operated by a simple sliding rod for opening or closing. Clean and lubricate these occasionally with powdered graphite.

Steel windows normally open and shut with a cranking mecha-nism. When repairs are necessary, check the gears first. To do this, loosen the set-screw on the handle and remove it. Then remove the two screws holding the gear box to the side of the window frame. Finally, remove the arm by sliding it along the slot until it lifts free. In some cases, you have to unscrew the hinged fitting that holds it.

Inspect the gears carefully. If they are dirty, clean them in gaso-line or other solvent that won't dam-age metal, then apply fresh grease. If the gears are worn and are not meshing smoothly, the whole mech-anism will have to be replaced. Large hardware stores or lumber-yards that sell casement windows can order one for you if they don't have it in stock. Take the old one with you so that exact measure-ments can be made.

For casement windows that do not close together tightly enough, you can shim behind the locking handle. Just remove it and then slip a shim under the plate. The handle, when reinstalled, will now draw the window sash up snug against the frame.

## Sliding Window

Sliding windows are largely main-tenance-free as long as the channel in which they slide is kept clean. If one of the rails is bent, correct it as you would for a sliding door (see page 88 for instructions).

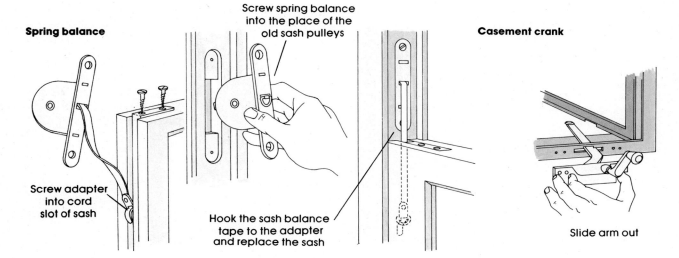

**Spring balance**

Screw adapter into cord slot of sash

Screw spring balance into the place of the old sash pulleys

Hook the sash balance tape to the adapter and replace the sash

**Casement crank**

Slide arm out

Any wood or steel surfaces on the house exterior must be kept protected from the elements; wood will soon rot, and metal will rust. Regular maintenance and touch-ups will markedly extend the life of doors and windows, both interior and exterior. Whether touching up or completely stripping and repainting wood doors and windows, don't forget all the edges. It is here that moisture can most easily penetrate and cause the wood to swell. Metal doors often have a baked enamel finish and should need little work other than touching up any chips.

Repainting wood doors and windows, especially if you first have to remove the old paint, is a boring and thankless job. But it will improve the appearance and life of the windows so much that it will prove worth the agony. So have at it. (For more information on interior painting, see Ortho's book, *Painting & Wallpapering*.)

## Wood

### Removing Old Paint

If the paint on the frame looks in reasonably good shape, go over it carefully for any blisters. Scrape the blister away, then sand the area until it is smooth. Lightly sand the paint on the sash and frame, then wipe clean.

If the paint is in poor condition—cracked and peeling away—it must be removed before you can paint. Simply painting over it will result in the new paint peeling away from the old.

The best tool for wide flat surfaces is a pull scraper, available at hardware stores. For narrow areas, use a flat-blade scraper. An easier way, albeit more expensive, is to use a paint remover. Brush on the remover, wait until the paint is softened, then peel it away. Use a putty knife to work under the paint and help lift it off. Any tough spots that remain must be scraped.

After the old paint is removed, sand the frame and sash with a coarse (90-grit) sandpaper to remove stubborn flakes. After all rough edges are removed, go over it again with a fine (180-grit) paper. Always sand with the wood grain. When you are finished, go over the frame with a damp cloth to remove all the sanding particles.

### Preparing the Wood

If there are any visible gouges in the wood, fill them in with a wood putty or spackling compound after sanding. Wood putty is applied directly from the can, while spackling compound—a dry powder—is first mixed with water to the consistency of a thick cream. If the gouge is deeper than ⅛ inch, fill it with two separate coats to prevent shrinkage. Use a putty knife to apply, and sand after each coat when dry.

### Doors

When you repaint a door, apply two coats of paint. The easiest way to paint a door is to take it off its hinges. Prop it against a wall or lay it across two sawhorses. Do not remove the hinges, but cover them with masking tape. If using oil-based paint, you can first lay on your coating with a roller, then spread it with a brush, as described below; if you are using latex, use a brush for the whole process.

First, using a roller, cover the door as well as you can. Work out from the middle, first up, then down. If the door is paneled, do the panels first.

Immediately after the rolling, spread and even out the paint with a 2-inch trim brush, following the grain of the wood. If the door is paneled, begin with the panels, painting the molding that frames them first. "Pull out" paint from inside corners by working the brush into the corner and pulling it out and away from the surface.

The latch edge of the door should match the room it opens into; the hinge edge should match the room it opens away from. Paint all edges. Paint the frame, working down from the top. Consult the illustration below to determine how much of the stop to paint.

**Painting a door**

Work out from the middle

"Pulling out" paint from corners

## Windows

Two coats of paint should always be applied: first the primer coat to seal and make the finish coat adhere, then the finish coat. The painting techniques, described below, are the same for both. If you are using latex paint, use latex primer; if you are using an oil-based paint, use an oil-based primer. Latex paint is the most widely used today on houses because it is high quality, cleans up with soap and water, and is cheaper than oil-based paints.

Choosing the right brush is another factor. For latex paint, use only synthetic bristles. Real bristles, which are stiff hairs from a hog, should be used only for oil-based paints. For window sashes and frames, a 3-inch-wide brush is usually sufficient. Buy the best: it will hold more paint and fewer bristles will dislodge and stick in the paint. On a good finish brush, the bristles are feathered (not all the same length) at the end rather than square cut. This allows you to press the brush down and paint a fine, clean edge.

Before painting, cover the glass beside the sash edge with strips of masking, transparent, or painter's tape, leaving a 1/16-inch gap of glass exposed. This allows the paint to form a complete watertight seal over the window putty. Since it is difficult to obtain that margin at the corners, put the tape in place, then cut it away with a utility knife to leave the 1/16-inch margin. Remove the tape immediately after the paint sets.

**Double-Hung Window.** To paint a double-hung window, open both sashes about 12 inches. Starting on the outside, paint the top portion of the inner window first, starting at the top and working down. Paint the exterior window and its bottom edge. Put the windows back to within about 2 inches of being closed and finish painting the interior window. Do not close them until completely dry. Move them a few inches several times during the drying period to prevent sticking.

After the window sash is done, paint the casing and trim, again working from the top to the bottom so you can pick up any drips and drops as you go.

The inside is painted in the same fashion, after first removing all hardware.

**Casement Window.** A wood casement window is painted in a straightforward fashion after you have removed all the hardware, except hinges, and applied masking tape. For a neat job around hinges, cover them with masking tape and then cut around the edges with a utility knife. Be careful not to paint any gear mechanisms.

## Steel & Aluminum

### Windows

Steel windows must be kept painted to prevent rust. Aluminum windows are not normally painted but can be finished with a protective coat of urethane if pitting is a problem in your area.

Steel windows should be sanded to bare metal before painting. A tough emery cloth works well here. Next, wash down the steel with white vinegar to clean the metal. This also helps paint adhere better. When the metal frame is dry, apply a metal primer coat, then put on the finish coat of metal formulated paint, which is usually oil-based.

### Doors

Most metal doors have a baked-enamel finish that should not require attention. You can touch up any chips in the finish by applying matching metal enamel paint.

**Painting a window**

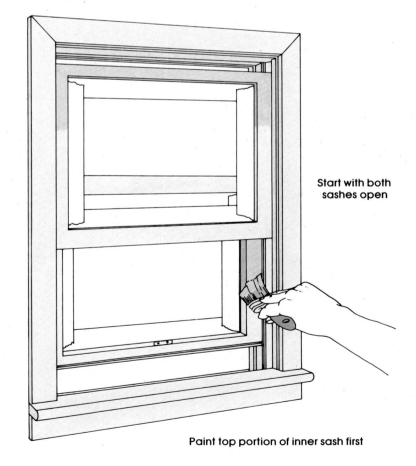

Start with both sashes open

Paint top portion of inner sash first

# INDEX

**A**

Acrylic glazing, 51
Acrylic latex caulk, 76
Airtightness
  importance of, 73
  testing for, 75
Aluminum flashing, 58
Aluminum-framed doors
  sliding glass, 32, 33
  storm and screen, 31
Aluminum-framed windows, 50.
  See also Metal-framed
  windows
  greenhouse, 61
  protective coating for, 93
  replacing glass in, 82
  replacing screening in, 83
  sliding, 43
Apron, 41, 51
  in curb flashing, 65
Astragal, 30
Awning or hopper windows,
  43, 50
  removing, 53
  weatherstripping, 81

**B**

Balloon-style house
  ceiling support for, 11
  framing door in, 14
  framing window in, 15
Base flashing, for skylight, 65
Bay windows
  alcoves for, 70–71
  choosing, 68
  installing, 68–69
Bearing walls, 10–11
Bifold doors, 17, 22, 23
  choosing, 36
  installing, 36
Blinds
  built-in, 43, 75
  for greenhouse windows,
  61
Brickmold, 40
Bristle sweep, 77
  installing, 78–79
Building codes
  on lumber, 6
  purpose of, 5
  window installation and,
  43
  on wiring, 12
Building permits, 5, 43
Butt hinges, 27
  thrust bearings for, 85
Butt joints, casing with, 41
Butyl glazing tape, 55, 56
Butyl rubber caulk, 76

**C**

Cap plate, 6, 7
  installing, 9
Carbide-tipped circular saw.
  See also Circular saw
  for cutting a door, 85
  for opening wall, 13
  for removing nailing-
  flange windows, 53
Carborundum blade, for
  cutting exterior wall, 15
Casement windows, 43, 50
  metal-framed, 53, 81, 82
  painting, 93
  removing, 53
  repairing, 91
  replacing glass in, 82
  sticking, 89
  weatherstripping, 81
  wood-framed, 81, 91
Casing, 40
Caulking
  air leaks, 75–76
  bay window, 69
  door sills, 26
  double doors, 30
  fixed windows, 56, 57
  greenhouse windows, 61
  materials for, 76
  metal-framed windows, 60
  skylights, 66
  sliding glass doors, 32, 33

threshold, 87
windows, 75, 76; see also
  specific types
Caulking gun, 76
Ceiling joists
  finding, 9
  nailing cap plate to, 9
Ceiling-support systems, 11
Chain, replacing sash cord
  with, 90
Circular saw
  for cutting door, 85
  for cutting exterior wall, 15
  for cutting siding, 85
  for cutting skylight
  opening, 64
  for installing threshold, 29
  for opening wall, 13
  for removing nailing-
  flange windows, 53
Cleaning windows, 43
Climate
  glass type and, 54
  skylight type and, 62
  window type and, 43, 80
Closet doors
  choosing, 17
  sliding, 37
Combination doors. See
  Storm and screen doors
Concrete floors, attaching
  stud wall to, 9
Condensation, storm
  windows and, 74
Coping a mitered joint, 40, 41
Cord pulley, 51
Corner studs, 7
Counter-weight systems, 58
  repairing, 90
Cripple studs
  above headers, 8, 9
  when opening wall, 13, 14
Cripple wall, around bay
  alcove, 71
Curb flashing, 65
Curb-mounted skylights, 62
  framing opening for, 62–64
  installing, 64–66
Cylinder locks, 38–39

**D**

Deadbolt lock, 38, 39
Design, 5
  doors as part of, 16, 17, 18–21
  trim as part of, 40
  windows as part of, 4, 43,
  44–47, 48–49
Door bucks, 27
  for repairing door, 85
Door casing, installing, 40–41
Door framing, 8
  in existing wall, 13–14
Door hinges
  installing, 27–28, 29
  repairing, 84–85
Door jambs
  constructing, 26
  flange stripping for, 77
  for double doors, 30
  installing, 26, 27, 29
  leaving room for, 8
  of prehung doors, 24–25
  of sliding glass doors,
  32–33
  shimming. See Shimming
  door jambs
Doorknobs, 38
Doors. See also specific types
  of doors
  altering existing openings
  for, 15
  choosing, 17, 22–23
  cutting, 85
  cutting exterior wall for, 15
  designing with, 16, 17,
  18–21
  exterior. See Exterior doors
  finishing, 29
  framing opening for, 8,
  13–14
  front, 16, 17, 18–19, 20, 22
  function of, 17
  hanging, 26–29

height of, 8
hinges on. See Hinges
ill-fitting, 84–86
installing, 24–29. See also
  specific types
  interior. See Interior doors
  knobs for, 38
  lock installation, 38–39
  planing to fit, 27, 85
  prehung, 23, 24–25, 30
  problem solving for, 84–88
  reducing air leaks around,
  75–79
  repainting, 92, 93
  repairing, 84–88
  replacing glass in, 82
  replacing threshold on,
  86–87
  sill installation, 26
  splintered, 88
  sticking, 84–85
  straightening, 86
  swollen wood in, 84
  trim for, 40–41
  trimming, 27, 85
  types of, 17, 22–23
  warped, 86
  weatherstripping, 75, 77,
  78–79
Door shoe, 77
  installing, 78, 79
Door sills, installing, 26
Door stops
  installing, 29
  moving, 86
Door sweep, 77
  for stopping air leaks, 75
  installing, 78–79
  on storm and screen door,
  31
Double doors, 22
  choosing, 30
  French, 20–21, 22
  installing, 30
  leaded glass, 21
Double-hung windows, 43, 50
  choosing, 58
  installing, 58–59
  parts of, 51
  removing, 52–53
  repainting, 93
  repairing, 90–91
  sticking, 89
  weatherstripping, 77, 80,
  81
Double-pane windows
  advantages of, 51, 54, 73,
  74
  buying, 54
  mini-blinds in, 43, 75
  rotating, 43
Double top plate.
  See Cap plate
Double-wall bubble sky-
  lights, 62
Drip edge, on bay window
  roof, 69
Drip groove, on window sill,
  55
Dutch doors, 20, 22

**E**

Electrical wiring, 5, 12, 43
Energy costs
  doors and, 17, 73
  dual windows and, 51, 54
  metal-framed windows
  and, 60
  single-pane windows and,
  51, 73
  sliding glass doors and, 32
  storm doors and, 31
  windows and, 5, 43, 73; see
  also specific types
Epoxy resin, for repairing
  plastic screens, 83
Exterior doors
  brickmold on, 40
  locks for, 38, 39
  prehung, 23, 24–25
  stops for, 29
  types of, 17, 22–23
  weatherstripping, 78–79

Exterior trim, 40
Exterior walls, cutting
  through, 15

**F**

Felt weatherstripping, 77, 81
Filler strips, 58, 59
Finishing doors, 29
Fire safety, locks and, 38
Fireblocks, prying up, 14, 15
Fixed-pane windows, 43, 50
  buying, 54
  caulking for, 80
  installing, 54–57
  metal-framed, removing,
  53
  replacing glass in, 82
Flanges, on storm and
  screen door, 31
Flange stripping, 77, 81
Flashing
  aluminum, around wood-
  framed window, 58
  for bay window roof, 69
  for curb-mounted skylight,
  65
  skylights require, 62
Flashing paper
  on door frame, 20, 30
  around metal-framed
  window, 60
  after removing window, 53
  around wood-framed
  window, 58
Floor, attaching stud wall to,
  9
Floor joists, for bay alcove,
  70–71
Flooring, for bay alcove, 71
Foam tape weatherstrip-
  ping, 77, 81
Frames, window, 50
Framing
  a bay window alcove, 71
  a bay window roof, 68–69
  determining type of, 10
  door openings, 8, 13–14; see
  also specific types of
  doors
  for double doors, 30
  for fixed-pane window,
  54–55
  a lightwell, 66–67
  for pocket door, 34
  skylight openings, 62–64, 66
  for sliding glass doors, 32
  window openings, 8, 9,
  54–55
French doors, 20–21, 22
Front doors, 16, 17, 18–19, 20,
  22

**G**

Gasket weatherstripping
  for threshold, 78, 79
  for windows, 81
GFCI (Ground Fault Circuit
  Interrupter), 12
Glass
  broken, replacing, 82
  for fixed-pane windows,
  54
  protecting during painting, 93
  types of, 51
Glass doors. See Sliding
  glass doors
Glazier's points, 82
Glazing, materials used for,
  51
Glazing compound, 82
Gluing door jambs, 27
Greenhouse windows, 61
  caulking for, 80
Ground Fault Circuit
  Interrupter (GFCI), 12

**H**

Head flashing, for skylight,
  65
Head jamb, of window, 51

Headers, 8
  size of, 8
  in skylight framing, 63, 64
  when opening wall, 13, 14, 15
Heat gain through windows,
  75
Hinges
  on double doors, 30
  fixing, 84–85
  installing, 27–28, 29
Hollow-core doors, 23
  bifold, 36
  fixing holes in, 87
  pocket, 34
  splintered, repairing, 88
  trimming, 85
Hopper windows. See
  Awning or hopper
  windows

**I**

Inside casing, 51
Inside stop, 51
Insulation
  for bay window roof, 69
  around doors, 76
  for lightwell, 67
  around windows, 74, 76
Interior doors
  casing around, 40
  leaded-glass, 21
  locks for, 38–39
  prehung, 23, 24–25
  types of, 17, 22, 23

**J**

Jack rafters, 63, 64
Jack studs. See Trimmer
  studs
Jalousie windows, 43, 50
  climate for, 43, 80
  removing, 53
Jamb extenders, 58, 59
Jambs. See Door jambs;
  Window jambs
Jig, for sawing doors, 85
Joists
  for bay window alcove,
  70–71
  ceiling, 9

**K**

Kickplate, on storm and
  screen door, 31
King studs, 8, 9
  in existing wall, 13, 14
Knee braces, 69
Knee wall, around bay
  alcove, 71

**L**

Latex caulk, 76
Latex paint, 93
Leaded-glass doors, 21
Ledger board (ribbon), 10
Lightwell (light shaft), 62
  constructing, 66–67
  cutting rafters for, 64
Lintels. See Headers
Lock nailing mitered joints,
  41
Lock stile, beveling inner
  edge of, 27
Locks
  installing, 38–39
  marking position of, 29
Louvered doors, bifold, 36
Lower sash, 51
Lower sash weight, 51
Lubricating windows, 89
Lumber
  for door jambs, 27
  for door sill, 26
  for headers, 8
  for stud walls, 6
  for window sill, 55
  for window stool, 41
  for window stops, 57

**M**

Maintenance
  doors, 84–88

importance of, 73
for window frame
    materials, 50
windows, 89–91
Meeting rails, 51
Metal doors
    exterior, 23
    fixing dents in, 88
    repainting, 92, 93
Metal door sweep, 77
Metal-framed windows, 50.
    See also Aluminum-framed
    windows
    bay, 68
    casement. See Casement
    windows
    choosing, 60
    greenhouse, 61
    installing, 60
    removing, 53
    repairing, 91
    repainting, 93
    replacing glass in, 82
    replacing wood-framed
    windows with, 60
Metal tension strip, 77
Mirrored sliding doors, 23
Mitered joints, on trim, 40–41
Molding
    as casing, 40, 41
    under door sill, 26
Mortise lock, 38, 39
Mortising for hinges, 27, 28
Mudsill, 10
Muntins, 51

N

Nailing-flange windows. See
    Metal-framed windows
Nail-on fins, 53
Nail protectors, for piping, 13
Nails
    for attaching wall to floor,
    9
    for installing door jambs,
    27
    for installing metal-framed
    window, 60
    for installing prehung
    door, 25
    for installing wood-framed
    window, 59
    setting, 40, 59
    for skylight framing, 64
    for stud wall construction,
    7
    for window framing, 9, 15
Neoprene rubber strips, for
    fixed-pane window, 57
Neoprene weatherstripping,
    77
Nylon bristle sweep, 77

O

Oil-based caulk, 76
Oil-based paint, 93
Openable windows, 43
Outside casing, 51
Outside stop, 51

P

Painting doors and windows,
    92–93
    for finishing, 29, 30
    after repair, 82
    trim on, 40
Parting bead, 51
Permits, 5, 43
Pipes, rerouting, 12–13
    permits for, 5, 43
Planing doors, 27, 85
Plastic filler, for metal doors,
    88
Plastic screens, repairing, 83
Plastic sheeting, 74, 75
Plate glazing, 51
Platform-style house, 10
    ceiling support for, 11
    framing door in, 13
    framing window in, 14–15
Plumber's tape, for bay
    window roof, 68, 69

Plumbing changes, 12–13
    permits for, 5, 43
Pocket doors, 17, 23
    choosing, 34
    installing, 34–35
Polyurethane caulk, 76
Polyurethane tape
    weatherstripping, 77
Porches, jalousie windows
    for, 43
Post-and-beam window
    framing, 54–55
Precut roof, for bay window,
    68–69
Prehung doors, 23
    doorknobs for, 38
    double, 30
    installing, 24–25
    three styles of, 24
    trimming, 25

R

Rabbet joints, for fixed-pane
    windows, 56, 57
Rafters
    for bay window roof, 68–69
    in skylight framing, 63
Rail, 51
Reciprocal saw, for cutting
    floor joists, 71
Reflective film, 75
Repainting doors and
    windows, 92–93
Repairing doors, 84–88
    hinges, 84–85
    hollow-core, 87, 88
    ill-fitting, 84–86
    metal, dented, 88
    replacing threshold, 86–87
    screen, 89
    sliding glass, 88
    splintered, 88
    warped or bowed, 86
Repairing windows, 89–91
    adjusting spring lift, 91
    casement, 91
    double-hung, 90–91
    replacing broken glass, 82
    replacing sash cord, 90
    screening, 83
    sliding, 91
    sticking, 89
Ribbon (ledger board), 10
Rim lock, 38
Roof, for bay window, 68–69
Rotating windows, 43, 50
    removing, 53
    weatherstripping, 81
Rough sill, 9
    for fixed window, 54, 55
    when opening wall, 15
Router
    for fixed-pane window
    installation, 57
    for hinge mortises, 28
Rubber caulking, 76
Rubber flange weatherstrip-
    ping, 77, 81

S

Saber saw, for cutting floor
    joists, 71
Saddle flashing, 65
Sanding sticking doors, 85
Sanding sealer. See Sealer
Sash cord, 51
    replacing, 90, 91
Sash parts, 51
Sash spring lift, adjusting, 91
Sash windows, replacing
    broken glass in, 82
Sawing a door, 85
Saw jig, for doors, 85
Screen doors, repairing, 88
Screening
    repairing or replacing, 83
    solar, 75
Sealer
    for door and window trim,
    40
    for finishing doors, 29, 30
    when replacing window
    glass, 82

Security
    doors function as, 17, 22
    locks for, 38, 39
    with sliding glass doors, 32
Self-flashing skylights, 62, 66
Setting nails, 40, 59
Shimming a bay window, 68
Shimming casement window
    handles, 91
Shimming door hinges, 84
    on double doors, 30
Shimming door jambs, 27, 29
    double doors, 30
    pocket door, 35
    sliding glass door, 33
    storm and screen doors, 31
Shimming door opening,
    24–25
Shimming fixed-pane
    window jambs, 57
Shimming window sills, 59
Shower doors, glazing for, 51
Silicone caulk, 76
Sills
    door, installing, 26
    window, 51. See also
    Rough sill
Single-hung windows, 43, 50
    wood-framed, installing,
    58–59
Single-pane windows, 51
    energy costs and, 73,
    stopping air leaks through,
    75
Skylights, 62–67
    caulking for, 80
    choosing, 62
    curb-mounted, 62–66
    locations for, 62
    self-flashing, 62, 66
    single-wall bubble, 62
Sliding doors, 23. See also
    Sliding glass doors
    closet, 37
    design function of, 17
    pocket, 34–35
Sliding glass doors, 17, 22
    bristle sweep for, 77
    choosing, 32
    glazing used for, 51
    installing, 32–33
    repairing bent rail in, 88
    replacing broken glass in,
    82
    weatherstripping for, 77
Sliding windows, 43, 50
    aluminum-framed, 43
    repairing, 91
    sticking, 89
    weatherstripping, 81
Solar screens, 75
Sole plate, 6, 7
Solid-core doors, 22, 23
Solid-panel doors, 22, 23
Soundproofing, doors for, 23
Spackling compound
    before painting doors or
    windows, 92
    for repairing door, 87
Sponge rubber weatherstrip-
    ping, 77, 81
Spring balance, replacing,
    91
Spring clips, in casement
    windows, 91
Spring lift, adjusting, 91
Squaring a wood-framed
    window, 58
Stain
    for door and window trim,
    40
    for finishing doors, 29, 30
Stained-glass windows, 51,
    54
Steel-framed windows, 50. See
    also Metal-framed
    windows
    casement, repairing, 91
    repainting, 93
Step flashing
    for bay window roof, 69
    for skylight, 65
Sticking doors, 84–85
Sticking windows, 89

Stile, 51
Stool, 41, 51
    of bay window, 68
Stops
    door, 29, 86
    no-jamb window installa-
    tion with, 56–57
Storm and screen doors, 22,
    74
    choosing, 31
    installing, 31
Storm windows
    energy costs and, 73
    installing, 74
    replacing broken glass in,
    82
Strip flashing, for bay
    window roof, 69
Structural changes, permits
    needed for, 5
Stud finder, 13
Studs
    cripple, 8, 9, 13, 14
    king, 8, 9, 13, 14
    locating, 13
    spacing for, 6
    trimmer (jack), 8, 9, 13, 14
    windows between, 54, 55
Stud wall construction, 6–9
Stud walls, temporary, 11
Synthetic rubber caulk, 76

T

Tempered glazing, 51
Tension strip, 77, 80, 81
Thermal barrier, glazing as,
    51
Thermal-break frames, 50,
    60
Thermal curtains, 75
Threshold
    of double doors, 30
    installing, 29, 79
    replacing, 86–87
    rubber, stopping air leaks
    with, 75
Threshold gasket, 77
    installing, 78, 79
Thrust bearings, 85
Top plate, 6, 7
Trim
    for doors, 40–41
    for prehung doors, 25
    weatherstripping around,
    76
    for windows, 40–41
Trimmer studs, 8, 9
    in existing wall, 13, 14
Trimming doors, 27, 85. See
    also Trim

U

Upper sash, 51
Upper sash weight, 51
Urethane foam caulk, 76

V

Veneer doors, repairing, 88
Ventilation
    with greenhouse windows,
    61
    with skylights, 62
    window type and, 43
Vinyl-clad windows, 50
Vinyl door shoe, 77
    installing, 79
Vinyl door sweep, 77
    installing, 78–79
Vinyl flange weatherstrip-
    ping, 77, 81
Vinyl latex caulk, 76
Vinyl tape weatherstripping,
    77
Vinyl tension strip, 77

W

Walls
    altering openings in, 15
    bearing vs. nonbearing,
    10–11
    building, 6–9
    cutting openings in, 10–15

cutting for pocket door, 34
    framing door opening in,
    13–14
    framing window openings
    in, 8, 9, 14–15, 54–55
    plumbing in, 12–13
    temporary support, 11
    wiring in, 12
Warped doors, repairing, 86
Weatherstripping
    allowing for, 27
    installing on doors, 78–79
    reasons for, 75
    testing, 75
    threshold, 29, 77, 78, 79
    types of, 77
    windows, 80–81
Weight pulleys, 51
Western framing. See Plat-
    form framing
Whaler, 11
Window casing, installing,
    40–41
Window framing, 8, 9
    in existing wall, 14–15
    for fixed-pane windows,
    54–55
Window insulation kit, 74
Window jambs, 51
    for fixed-pane windows,
    56–57
    flange stripping for, 77
    jamb extenders, 58, 59
Windows. See also Skylights;
    specific types of windows
    altering existing openings
    for, 15
    anatomy of, 51
    bay, 68–71
    caulking, 75, 76
    cleaning, window type
    and, 43
    cutting exterior wall for, 15
    designing with, 4, 44–47,
    48–49
    fixed vs. openable, 43
    framing. See Window
    framing
    function of, 43, 73
    greenhouse, 61
    installing, 54–61
    measuring for replace-
    ment of, 52
    painting, 92, 93
    reducing heat gain
    through, 75
    reducing heat loss
    through, 74–77, 80–81
    removing, 52–53
    repairing, 82–83, 89–91
    replacing broken glass in,
    82
    sticking, 89
    trimming, 40–41
    types of, 43, 50
    for ventilation, 43
    weatherstripping, 75, 80–81
Window sill, 51
    drip groove on, 55
    for fixed window, install-
    ing, 55
Window walls, 4
Wire screens, repairing, 83
Wiring changes, 12
    permits for, 5, 43
Wood doors, repainting, 92
    hollow-core. See Hollow-
    core doors
    solid-core, 22, 23
    solid-panel, 22, 23
Wood-framed screens, re-
    placing screening in, 83
Wood-framed windows, 50
    bay, 68
    casement. See Casement
    windows
    choosing, 58
    installing, 58–59
    removing, 52–53
    replacing glass in, 82
    replacing with metal-
    framed, 60
Wood putty, for finishing trim,
    40

# METRIC CHART

## U.S. Measure and Metric Measure Conversion Chart

| | Symbol | When you know: | Multiply by: | To find: | | | **Rounded Measures for Quick Reference** | | |
|---|---|---|---|---|---|---|---|---|---|
| **Mass (Weight)** | oz | ounces | 28.35 | grams | 1 oz | | | = | 30 g |
| | lb | pounds | 0.45 | kilograms | 4 oz | | | = | 115 g |
| | g | grams | 0.035 | ounces | 8 oz | | | = | 225 g |
| | kg | kilograms | 2.2 | pounds | 16 oz | = | 1 lb | = | 450 g |
| | | | | | 32 oz | = | 2 lb | = | 900 g |
| | | | | | 36 oz | = | 2-1/4 lb | = | 1000 g |
| | | | | | | | | | (1 kg) |
| **Volume** | tsp | teaspoons | 5 | milliliters | 1/4 tsp | = | 1/24 oz | = | 1 ml |
| | tbsp | tablespoons | 15 | milliliters | 1/2 tsp | = | 1/12 oz | = | 2 ml |
| | fl oz | fluid ounces | 29.57 | milliliters | 1 tsp | = | 1/6 oz | = | 5 ml |
| | c | cups | 0.24 | liters | 1 tbsp | = | 1/2 oz | = | 15 ml |
| | pt | pints | 0.47 | liters | 1 c | = | 8 oz | = | 250 ml |
| | qt | quarts | 0.95 | liters | 2 c (1 pt) | = | 16 oz | = | 500 ml |
| | gal | gallons | 3.785 | liters | 4 c (1 qt) | = | 32 oz | = | 1 l |
| | ml | milliliters | 0.034 | fluid ounces | 4 qt (1 gal) | = | 128 oz | = | 3-3/4 l |
| **Length** | in. | inches | 2.54 | centimeters | 3/8 in. | | | = | 1 cm |
| | ft | feet | 30.48 | centimeters | 1 in. | | | = | 2.5 cm |
| | yd | yards | 0.9144 | meters | 2 in. | | | = | 5 cm |
| | mi | miles | 1.609 | kilometers | 12 in. (1 ft) | | | = | 30 cm |
| | km | kilometers | 0.621 | miles | 1 yd | | | = | 90 cm |
| | m | meters | 1.094 | yards | 100 ft | | | = | 30 m |
| | cm | centimeters | 0.39 | inches | 1 mi | | | = | 1.6 km |
| **Temperature** | F° | Fahrenheit | 5/9 | Celsius | 32°F | | | = | 0°C |
| | | | (after subtracting 32) | | 68°F | | | = | 20°C |
| | C° | Celsius | 9/5 | Fahrenheit | 212°F | | | = | 100°C |
| | | | +32 | | | | | | |
| **Area** | in.$^2$ | square inches | 6.452 | square centimeters | 1 in.$^2$ | | | = | 6.5 cm$^2$ |
| | | | | | 1 ft$^2$ | | | = | 930 cm$^2$ |
| | ft$^2$ | square feet | 929 | square centimeters | 1 yd$^2$ | | | = | 8360 cm$^2$ |
| | | | | | 1 a | | | = | 4050 m$^2$ |
| | yd$^2$ | square yards | 8361 | square centimeters | | | | | |
| | a | acres | .4047 | hectares | | | | | |

Proof-of-Purchase
0-89721-023-9